25 WALKS

THE
TROSSACHS

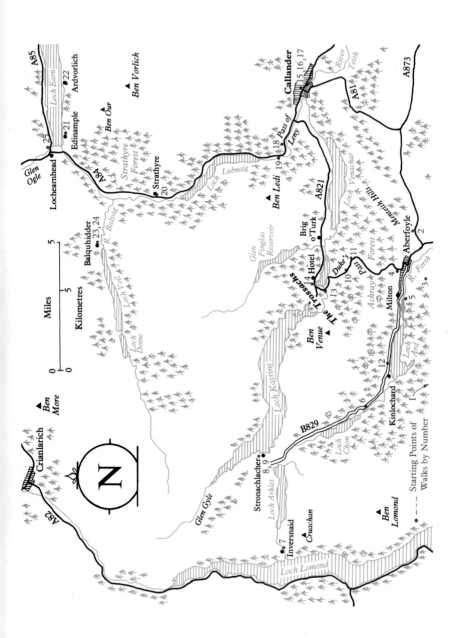

25 WALKS

THE TROSSACHS

Cameron McNeish

Series Editor: Roger Smith

A partnership organisation linking the three District Councils of Clackmannan, Dumbarton and Stirling, the Scottish Tourist Board and the local Tourist Trade.

EDINBURGH:HMSO

Applications for reproduction should be made to HMSO

Acknowledgements

Thanks are due to the following:
The Loch Lomond, Stirling and Trossachs Tourist Board for their help
in the preparation of the text and for the supply of cover and
additional transparencies.
The Scottish Wildlife Trust for access to their transparencies.

British Library Cataloguing in Publication Data

A catalogue record for this book is available from the British Library

ISBN 0 11 495166 7

CONTENTS

USEFUL INFORMATION

The length of each walk is given in kilometres and miles, but within the text measurements are metric for simplicity. The walks are described in detail and are supported by accompanying maps (study them before you start the walk), so there is little likelihood of getting lost, but if you want a back-up you will find the 1:25 000 Pathfinder Ordnance Survey maps on sale locally.

Every care has been taken to make the descriptions and maps as accurate as possible, but the author and publishers can accept no responsibility for errors, however caused. The countryside is always changing and there will inevitably be alterations to some aspects of these walks as time goes by. The publishers and author would be happy to receive comments and suggested alterations for future editions of the book.

Abbreviations
A number of abbreviations are used within the text. Usually these are explained, but a few, used frequently, are explained here.

NTS: The National Trust for Scotland. NTS has in its care over 100 properties of all kinds, ranging from small vernacular cottages and individual landscape features to great houses and large areas of superb mountain country.

OS: Ordnance Survey. The OS is our national mapping agency, covering the whole of the UK at various scales. The two scales most frequently used by walkers are 1:25 000 and 1:500 000. All OS maps are drawn on a grid of kilometre squares.

RSPB: Royal Society for the Protection of Birds. The largest conservation body of its kind in the UK with a membership approaching one million.

SNH: Scottish Natural Heritage. The government's conservation agency in Scotland. Formed in 1992 by a merger of the former Nature Conservancy Council and the Countryside Commission for Scotland, SNH has a remit covering scientific research, habitat conservation, access and recreation.

METRIC MEASUREMENTS

At the beginning of each walk, the distance is given in miles and kilometres. Within the text, all measurements are metric for simplicity (and indeed our Ordnance Survey maps are now all metric). However, it was felt that a conversion table might be useful to those readers who, like the author, still tend to think in Imperial terms.

The basic statistic to remember is that one kilometre is five-eighths of a mile. Half a mile is equivalent to 800 metres and a quarter-mile is 400 metres. Below that distance, yards and metres are little different in practical terms.

km	miles
1	0.625
1.6	1
2	1.25
3	1.875
3.2	2
4	2.5
4.8	3
5	3.125
6	3.75
6.4	4
7	4.375
8	5
9	5.625
10	6.25
16	10

INTRODUCTION

The Trossachs have been described as 'the Highlands in miniature'. The very name tends to conjure up images of lochs, crag-girt mountains, bluffs and heather hollows, mountain slopes swathed in rich forest and a rich and abundant wildlife – a compressed portrayal of all those qualities which make the Scottish highlands so renowned throughout the world.

But this wasn't always a loved land, a welcoming land. Before the 19th century this was a land 'beyond the border', a district sequestered from the laws of the day and ruled and dictated to by an ancient Clan system. Travellers were not welcome, and foraging parties of clansmen would regularly plunge south into the lowlands on excursions of robbery and mayhem.

And yet, by the time the Jacobite uprisings were over, by the time the clan system was brought under control, adventurous travellers were taking advantage of the new-found freedom (and better roads) to penetrate north of the Highland Line without danger. By the time the 19th century came round, the Trossachs were quickly becoming Scotland's first tourist region.

'So wondrous wild, the whole might seem, The scenery of a faery dream.' So wrote Sir Walter Scott, one of the first enthusiastic travel writers to visit the area and spread the good news. Others followed, and soon the Trossachs were famous at home and abroad. Countless writers, poets, artists and those who just enjoy beautiful places have been drawn to its quiet glens and rugged tops, fascinated by the tales of Rob Roy and the Macgregors. But the history of the place was fascinating even before the birth of Rob Roy Macgregor. Britons, Erse, Celts, Scots, Picts and even Romans have all left their mark on the landscape of the Trossachs and have left a rich tapestry of culture.

Today, tourists can enjoy the quiet roads – you can even drive through the solitude of some of the great forests. Many enjoy these forest trails by mountain bike, while most still enjoy the traditional method of exploring on foot. And there is plenty to explore. Ancient woodland, modern forests, tranquil lochsides, Victorian industrial architecture and finest of all – the mountain tops, where the eyes can wander over hundreds of miles of gorgeous landscape, where you can walk unrestricted, the wind caressing your upturned face. There is history here, and great beauty. I hope you enjoy following these walks as much as I have enjoyed writing them.

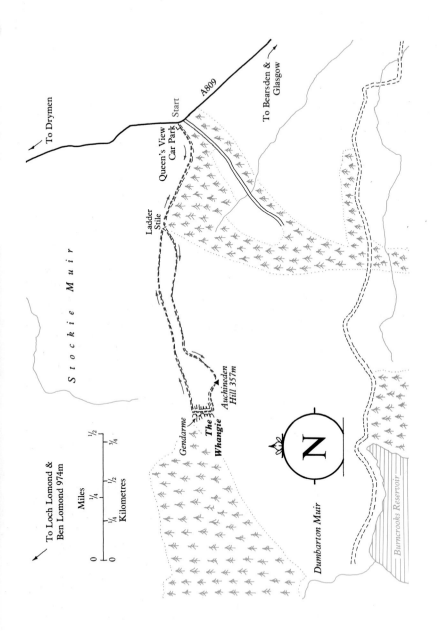

To Drymen

Stockie Muir

To Loch Lomond &
Ben Lomond 974m

Miles
0   ¼   ½   ¾   1
0   ¼   ½   ¾   1
Kilometres

A809

Queen's View
Car Park

Start

To Bearsden &
Glasgow

Ladder
Stile

Gendarme

The
Whangie

Auchineden
Hill 357m

N

Dumbarton Muir

Burncrooks Reservoir

THE WHANGIE

Although not strictly within the borders of the Trossachs, the geological phenomenon of the Whangie has long been associated with that district, sitting as it does on the brow of Auchineden Hill overlooking Stockie Muir towards Loch Lomond and the rising ground of the Trossachs hills.

The short walk from the Queen's View car park on the A809 Glasgow to Drymen road has long been a favourite with walkers, and sunny summer evenings and Sunday afternoons see dozens of visitors drive from Glasgow for a wee stroll to the Whangie. It's been a popular destination for generations and as long ago as the end of last century, Hugh MacDonald, writing in Glasgow's *Evening Citizen*, described it as a good walk. His description of the Whangie itself as a 'vast section of the hill that has by some means been wrenched asunder, leaving a lengthened and deepened chasm yawning along the line of separation' must have caught the public's imagination!

It's a good description of the feature. Imagine a smooth hillside, easy-angled with tussocky grass. At the far end of this ordinary hill, as though by some malevolent force, a section has been pulled away, leaving a long and narrow ravine between it and the original hillside. The edges of both parts of the hill form a savage

INFORMATION

Distance: 5 km (3 miles).

Start and finish: The car park known as the Queen's View, on the A809 Glasgow to Drymen road, about 11 km north of Bearsden, 10 km south of Drymen.

Terrain: All of the walk is on a path which can become very wet and muddy after heavy rain. The return route along the foot of the hill can become particularly boggy so good boots or wellies are recommended. Not really a walk for trainers, other than in very dry weather.

Refreshments: None. Nearest cafés, pubs, etc., are in Drymen and Croftamie.

View from the Whangie.

pinnacled crest, and as Hugh MacDonald pointed out in his article published over 100 years ago, 'the projections of one side (of the ravine) correspond with singular exactness to the hollows of the other'.

It's been claimed that this phenomenon was the work of the devil. After hosting a particularly successful meeting of witches and warlocks somewhere on the Kilpatrick Hills, he was flying to another meeting near Dumbarton when, feeling rather pleased with himself, he flicked his tail in jubilation, tearing apart the hillside over which he was flying.

View from the Whangie.

The truth is less sinister but equally melodramatic. It's believed that the feature of the Whangie is the result of 'glacial plucking', the action created by extreme temperatures which froze the rock slabs to the glacier. As the glacier began to move, it 'plucked' the hillside, causing a fracture to form. In effect, it tore the hillside apart, creating the long and sinuous cavern between the two sections.

At the Queen's View car park, an interpretive sign offers a good explanation of the geological features of the area. Go through a gap in the wall and follow the obvious path uphill towards a stand of conifers. Near the top of the hill cross over a ladder stile.

Here you have a choice of paths. The upper path follows a route along the top of the northern escarpment of Auchineden Hill to the trig point at its western end. A lower path runs along the hillside at the foot of this escarpment and offers a level of protection from the weather if the wind is blowing. At the far end of the hill both paths converge, and continue to the trig point on the summit of the 357 m/1170 ft Auchineden Hill.

This is a good spot to sit awhile and survey the prospect around you, taking in the wild flats of the Dumbarton and Stockie Muirs, the Kilpatrick Hills to the south, and the glistening waters of Loch Lomond to the north-west. The obvious big hill to the north is Ben Lomond, Scotland's most southerly Munro (hill over 914 m/3000 ft), and to the right of Ben Lomond lie the jumbled hills of the Trossachs themselves.

Take the path from the summit in a westerly direction and drop down to more broken ground, looking out for the crags which begin to appear on your right. Soon the path seems to go inside the rock face itself, and in essence that is exactly what it does. Follow it and you'll find yourself inside the Whangie with rock walls rising sheer on either side of you.

The cleft is about 100 m in length and rises on both sides to a height of 13 m. A one point in the sinuous depths, the walls are less than a metre apart, emphasising a feeling of claustrophobia!

Follow the path through the cleft, exiting past a smaller flake at the northern end known at the Gendarme. This smaller feature, and the walls of the Whangie itself, have been popular with rock climbers over the generations, but the recent explosion in rock climbing standards has been most climbers go off in search of harder, more extreme problems, and the Whangie is little used by the rock gymnasts nowadays.

Go past the Gendarme, taking the lowest path, and follow it back along the foot of the hill, all the way back to the ladder stile, and the downhill path to the Queen's View, which is named after a visit by Queen Victoria in 1879.

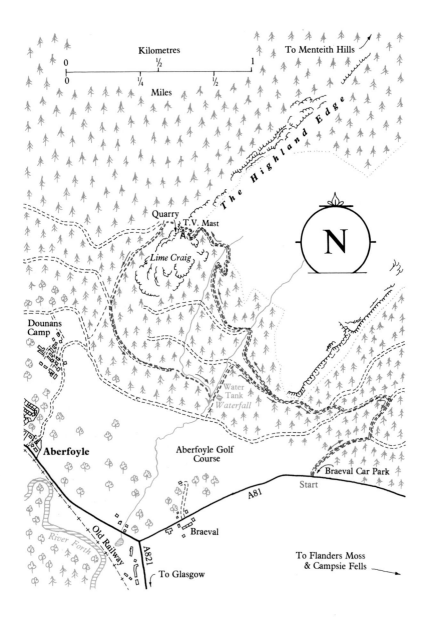

THE HIGHLAND EDGE

Less than 30 miles from the centre of Glasgow, the village of Aberfoyle is on the very edge of the Highlands. Indeed, the village sits on the geological Highland Fault Line which runs across Scotland from the south end of Loch Lomond to Stonehaven on the north-east coast.

The clans who inhabited the regions north of this line were, until comparatively recently, as Sir Walter Scott so succinctly puts it, 'much addicted to predatory excursions upon their Lowland neighbours'. As such, Aberfoyle has a turbulent history. Graham's *Sketches of Scenery in Perthshire* published in 1806, explains; 'Tis well known, that in the highlands, it was in former times accounted not only lawful, but honourable, among hostile tribes, to commit depredations on one another; and these habits of the age were perhaps strengthened in this district by the circumstances which have been mentioned. It bordered on a country, the inhabitants of which, while they were richer, were less warlike than they, and widely differenced by language and manners.'

This walk, on to the Highland Edge itself, certainly emphasises the geographic difference between those districts to the north and to the south of this geological faultline. The views to the south cross some of the flattest land in all Scotland, Flanders Moss, towards the lowland hills of the Campsies. Northwards, a jumble of high hills and mountains dominate, a different land entirely.

From the Braeval car park, head uphill on the broad forest track. At the first junction turn left, and 200 m further on you'll reach a second junction. The track which goes straight on leads over the Menteith Hills to Callander, but our route goes to the left, marked by a signpost with a white painted arrow. Follow the track steadily uphill through a forest of larches; the slopes on both sides are covered in bracken and in season, bright yellow gorse and whin.

After another 200 m turn right, following the signpost to Lime Craig. As you climb steadily up the hill, views begin to open up on your left across the broad expanse

INFORMATION

Distance: 6 km (4 miles).

Start and finish: Braeval car park, on A81 1.5 km east of Aberfoyle.

Terrain: Mostly on forest tracks but some narrow footpaths which are inclined to become muddy after wet weather. Steady uphill for the first part of the walk and some steeper downhill sections on the return.

Waymarked: Partly.

Time: Allow a good 2½–3 hours.

Points of Interest:
1. The view from the Highland Edge on the summit of Lime Craig.
2. The limestone quarry to the north of Lime Craig.
3. The line of the old incline railway which took the lime down to the lime kilns at the foot of the hill. Look out for deer, both red and roe, peregrine falcons, squirrels.

Refreshments: None en route. Wide selection in Aberfoyle.

of Flanders Moss towards the distant Campsie Fells. Here and there you'll spot the buildings in Aberfoyle through the trees. Continue for about 300m when you'll reach another junction; this time take the right fork, continuing uphill. High up on the hill to your right are some crags, and as I researched this walk I heard the distinct call of a peregrine falcon. Keep your eyes peeled hereabouts for a sight of this remarkable bird of prey, the fastest bird that lives in this country.

Highland Boundary Fault.

This is a pleasant part of the forest, with open rides offering distant views and some scattered rowans breaking the monotony of conifers. Soon you'll reach a prominent bend in the track as it crosses a noisy little stream. This is a good spot to stop for a bit of a break on the long climb to the summit of Lime Craig. Just beyond the bend, ignore the track which branches off to the left. Continue uphill yet again, but take heart, as you round the next bend you'll see the TV mast and hut which sit on the summit of Lime Craig, your destination.

I was surprised to see a red deer hind as I climbed up here; it's much more common to see the smaller roe deer in these forests. The red deer was originally a forest dweller when much of the Scottish highlands was still covered in Caledonian Pine forest. But as man systematically cleared the forests over the centuries, the red deer took to the high bare slopes of the mountains, where they tend to live now, eking sustenance from the scarce vegetation. It's always good to see them in the forest, their natural habitat.

As the track begins to wind round towards the summit the views open up and there is a very real sense of being on the edge of the highlands, for you are standing on the Highland Line, the geological fault which runs across Scotland.

Although the television mast and hut on the summit take away the feeling of wildness from the scene, the views around are still stunning. To the south you look over Flanders Moss to the distant Fintry Hills and Campsie Fells – to the west out over Aberfoyle itself with the David Marshall Lodge and its lochan sitting proudly on its wooded knoll; north to Ben Venue over a sea of green conifers.

A few metres from the summit on the north side you'll see a signpost, a white arrow and blue dot – this indicates the descent route. Initially the path is peaty and a bit boggy, then wooden steps descend steeply to the woods. The track is quite eroded in places, so take care.

Track from summit towards the old conglomerate quarry.

As you descend, look to your left where you'll see the hollow of the old limestone quarry from which Lime Craig takes its name. Leave the track and go into the quarry where a series of interpretive signs explain the geology of the area and point out examples of limestone, and the strange conglomerate, descriptively known as 'pudding stone'.

Leave the quarry, pass a wooden bench on the right and take the footpath which leads off to the left. This path follows the line of the original incline railway which transported lime from the quarry down to the lime kilns at the foot of the hill. After about 500 m on this footpath you come across a wide forest track. Immediately across the track a blue waymarker points out the route down to Dounans Camp at Aberfoyle. You can go this way, but a more interesting route goes to the left, along the forest track to its termination point where a narrow footpath begins.

Follow this footpath as it weaves its way through the trees, crossing the stream, then slightly lower down cross back over to its right bank. The path is very sketchy hereabouts but follow the line of the stream for a few metres until you see a prominent waterfall. You can cross the stream quite easily above the fall, and climb the steep bank to meet another track just below a Central Regional Council Water Department water tank. Turn left onto this track and follow it past the water tank, where it climbs quite steeply for a good 400 m. At its junction with a wide forestry track turn right and 200 m later this track merges with the track which runs back to Braeval.

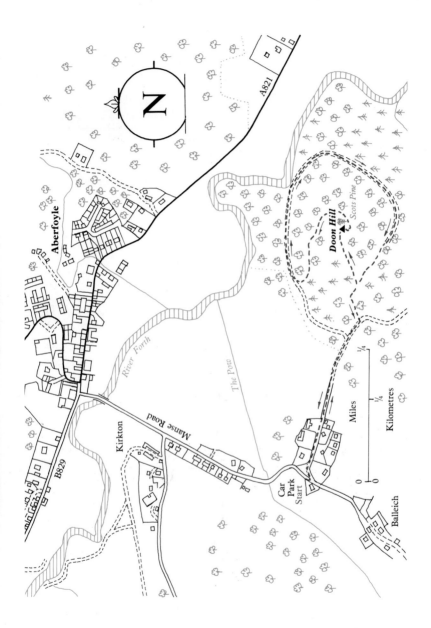

THE FAIRIES OF DOON HILL

While Aberfoyle, with its Bailie Nicol Jarvie inn, is strongly associated with Sir Walter Scott and Rob Roy, there is another remarkable, though less well known, character who also has strong links with the village. The Reverend Robert Kirk was the seventh son of Aberfoyle's parish minister, and later became minister of Aberfoyle himself. He was also, at one time, minister of Balquhidder.

Kirk was convinced of the existence of fairies, and indeed in 1691 wrote an amazing book called *The Secret Commonwealth of Elves, Faunes and Fairies*. It is believed that Kirk was walking one day on Doon Hill, close to the Aberfoyle manse, when he sank to the ground, apparently dead. Shortly after his funeral, he reappeared as a ghost, and explained, 'I fell down in a swoon, and was carried into fairyland, where I am now.'

INFORMATION

Distance: 3 km (2 miles).

Start and finish: Forestry Commission parking place at Balleich, a mile or so from Aberfoyle along Manse Road.

Terrain: Forest tracks and footpaths which can be muddy after wet weather. Boots or wellies recommended.

Time: Give yourself an hour or so but take your time in the oakwoods searching for the fairy people!

Points of interest: Lovely Scots Pine on the summit of the hill, magnificent oak woods, and the coppice woods towards the end of the walk. Look out for roe deer, grey squirrels, chiffchaff, chaffinches, treecreepers, blackbird, cuckoo, wood pigeons.

Refreshments: Hotels, cafes, restaurants and a fish and chip shop in Aberfoyle. There are also public toilets in Aberfoyle.

Track from the summit of Doon Hill through pine woods.

It was sincerely believed by many of his parishioners at the time that Kirk was indeed a captive of the fairy people, and that his spirit was held within the confines of an old Scots Pine tree on the summit of Doon Hill. This walk takes us to that summit, but is a fine short walk in its own right, with a lovely climb up through some magnificent oak woods.

Doon trail signposts.

The Fairy Walk is well signposted by signs bearing toadstools! Follow the tarmac road to its end where it merges into a forestry track with open meadows to your left. Aberfoyle lies across the river flats backed by the hills of the Highland Edge with the David Marshall Lodge clearly visible high above the village. Doon Hill lies ahead.

As you enter the woods, pass a track on the left and continue uphill for 50 m to a sign which indicates Doon Hill Fairy Walk. Immediately opposite, a path leads off through the trees. Follow this path, and from here to the summit enjoy its tranquillity as it wends it way through magnificent natural woods of oak, birch and holly.

Look out for chiffchaff, treecreepers, chaffinches, blackbirds and wood pigeons. You may be lucky too and spot grey squirrels leaping from bough to bough. The path winds its way steadily up the hill and comes suddenly to the flat summit which is crowned by a magnificent Scots Pine; said to be the tree which contains the spirit of Robert Kirk!

Begin the descent by following the toadstool signpost, down through the oaks. I walked this route early one June morning with the sunlight filtering through the green canopy overhead; it really did feel like a fairyland.

At the foot of the hill, as the path levels out and enters a fringe of larches, leave the narrow footpath and drop down to your right where, in about 20–30 m, you'll come across a forestry track which in fact runs around the base of Doon Hill. By leaving the official *Fairy Walk* at this point, your walk is lengthened by a kilometre or so and offers a pleasant detour around the base of the hill. You can of course choose to follow the Fairy Walk to the end which gives you a walk of about 1.5 km.

Magic mushrooms.

On reaching the forestry track, turn right along it with birches on your left and the oakwoods shrouding the hillside to your right. After a couple of hundred metres you'll pass the River Forth on your left, still in its infancy after its run down from the foot of Ben Lomond. The Forth is one of Scotland's most important rivers, meeting the sea at the Firth of Forth between Fife and Lothian.

Continue following the track; after a lovely open section of the walk the path re-enters the trees again and at a Mountain Bike signpost the broad forest track narrows into a footpath, which becomes quite muddy in places. This footpath now runs through woods of a very different character. Instead of the majestic oak woods or the suffocating conifer plantations the path now goes through an oak coppice, where the trees have been regularly cut to produce young straight trees which, in former days, would have been coppiced at regular intervals.

After a while the path turns sharply left, up a bank, and through a lovely open meadow. Cross the meadow and as you enter the trees again turn immediately to your right on to the track which takes you back to your starting point.

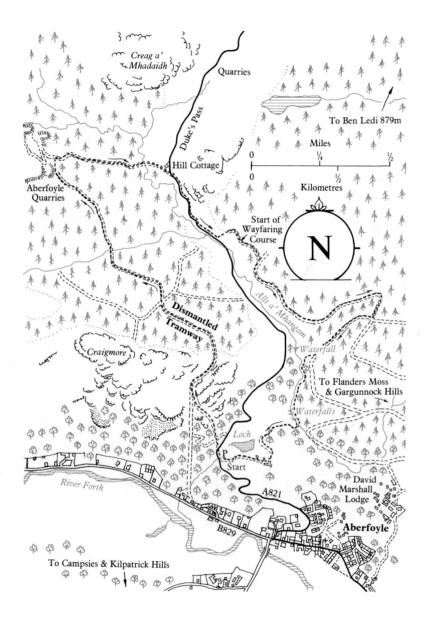

TRAMWAYS OF THE TROSSACHS

Aberfoyle is situated on the southern edge of the 42000 acre Queen Elizabeth Forest Park, a huge area in which the Forestry Commission has largely succeeded in combining commercial forestry with recreation, with miles of signposted footpaths for walkers and cyclists. You can even drive through some of the forest roads which are specially open for motorists.

At the south side of the Park, on a hillside above Aberfoyle, lies the David Marshall Lodge. This was built by the Carnegie Trust of which David Marshall was chairman, as a viewpoint and picnic area. It was later gifted to the Forestry Commission, who use it today as an information centre for the Forest Park. There is a large car park, picnic areas, a pleasant loch and a myriad forest trails offering some delightful walks and viewpoints south over the low-lying lands of the infant Forth to the distant Campsies and Kilpatrick hills.

To the north-west of the Lodge, the hills of Creagmore and Creag a' Mhadaidh are broken up by large quarries. These old slate quarries were once the third largest of their type in Scotland and provided considerable employment in Aberfoyle. A tramway linked the top quarries adjacent to the road known as the Duke's Pass, named after the Duke of Montrose, all the way downhill to the old railway station in Aberfoyle itself. But the quarrying of slate wasn't Aberfoyle's only industry. It was once the centre of an iron smelting industry.

About halfway round this walk the route crosses over the Duke's Pass, once the scene of intense combat in 1651 when Oliver Cromwell's lieutenant in Scotland, General Monck, tried to subdue Royalist forces. Trouble flared two years later again when the Earl of Glencairn and Graham of Duchray ambushed Monck's men, this time routing the Cromwellian force. There are some fine waterfalls near the end of the walk as you return to the David Marshall Lodge.

From the entrance to the David Marshall Lodge car park, turn right on to the main road and about 50m further on you'll notice a narrow footpath leaving the road on the left. Follow this footpath steeply uphill through the bracken. Continue uphill, ignoring a level track which

INFORMATION

Distance: 7 km (4 miles).

Start and finish: David Marshall Lodge, 2 km north of Aberfoyle on A821.

Terrain: A fairly easy and straightforward walk after a steep start but take care as you approach the quarry workings just south of the main Aberfoyle Quarry. Boots or wellies are advised.

Time: Give yourself about 3 hours and take some time if you can to enjoy some of the shorter trails in the grounds of the David Marshall Lodge.

Refreshments: Tea room in David Marshall Lodge. Cafés, fish and chip shops, restaurants and pubs in Aberfoyle.

Toilets: In the David Marshall Lodge.

crosses the path after 50 m, and shortly after that cross a fence by means of a stile.

With your heart pumping and legs aching, you'll no doubt notice that this is quite a steep and energetic start to the walk, so take your time, stopping now and again to enjoy the views which are opening up behind you over the David Marshall Lodge and across Flanders Moss to the Gargunnock and Fintry hills.

The David Marshall Lodge.

You soon reach the old tramway, where your uphill path reaches a pile of rubble and old slate. A much more level path continues to the right around the shoulder of the hill, where you'll enjoy good views across the Duke's Pass to our Highland Boundary Walk. In front of you lies a forestry plantation, so go through the handy gap in the fence (at the time of writing the stile had fallen down) and continue along the tramway. As you wander through the woods, wrestling from time to time with storm damaged fallen trees, you'll notice through the various clearings to your right that you've suddenly moved from lowland scenery to highland hills, one of the dramatic features of this whole area. Ben Ledi lies in the distance, with the Duke's Pass winding its way through the hills below you.

After 20 minutes or so of following the obvious tramway track through the woods, you'll reach a section where old quarry workings have forced the path into a series of zig-zags through the dense conifer plantations. Take great care as the path edge is liable to crumble. Stick carefully to the path and don't be tempted to down-climb into any of the old quarry workings – it's all very loose and dangerous!

At the fourth of these old workings, you'll come across an old cable wind, now very rusty and dilapidated. Shortly after this you'll reach the main quarry – bend slightly right, cross a small stream and follow the main quarry access road to the right down to Hill Cottage, which sits beside the Duke's Pass road. The slate in the quarry tends to be unstable, particularly after rain, and it's unwise to scramble about in the quarry itself.

A rusting artefact from the earlier slate industry.

At the cottage turn right and follow the main road for 400 metres.

Turn left into the forest at a sign which indicates the start of a wayfaring course, and follow the forest track, bearing right and past the start of the wayfaring route. Turn right at the first junction you come to, and continue on this new track, in time passing an area of clear fell before the path curves tightly to the right.

As you come off the bend, go right at the obvious cross-roads, down a pleasant curved track with larches on your right and a tinkling burn on the left. Watch out for this burn going under the forest track, because shortly after that you'll see a marker post (blue dot) on the right of the track. Follow this footpath down to some lovely small waterfalls.

From these falls, follow the path back over another narrow burn and up a bank where there is a signpost which proclaims the message that GEOLOGY IS DYNAMIC! Turn right at the top of the bank, beside the signpost, and follow the path along the top of the bank, under lovely oaks and larches. Take care hereabouts, as the burn on your right, the Allt a' Mhangam, the 'stream of the little fawn', suddenly flows into a deep steep-sided gorge, dropping over some big rocky steps to form a series of impressive waterfalls.

The reed-covered lochan in the David Marshall Lodge car park.

Return to the forest track and at a marker post turn right and re-enter the valley of the burn. Continue through some oak and holly woodland and cross the footbridge below the waterfall. Turn right and follow the trails, signposts and timber sculptures back to the David Marshall Lodge car park.

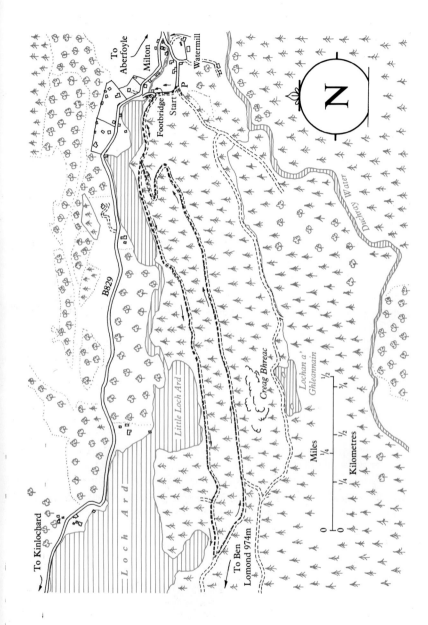

To Aberfoyle
Milton
Watermill
Footbridge
Start
P
To Kinlochard
B829
Loch Ard
Little Loch Ard
Creag Bhreac
Lochan a' Ghleamain
Duchray Water
To Ben Lomond 974m

N

Miles
¼   ¼   ½
0
Kilometres
¼   ½   ¾
0

LOCH ARD

This walk is mostly on wide forest tracks, climbing easily to a high point which offers a fine view over Loch Ard, a real jewel of a loch, towards distant Ben Lomond. Although the forestry is less varied than in other walks in this guide, it is a worthwhile outing for an evening stroll when the sun is beginning to sink in the west, silhouetting Ben Lomond and the hills beyond.

From the car park, go back to the information sign. Turn left at the signpost and go through a gate. Pass the stepping stones and footbridge which cross the stream and continue on the path past the cottage which is called Lochend. This initial stretch of the walk is a lovely tranquil section with views across the loch to a reed fringed distant shore.

At a junction of paths go right, waymarked by red and blue loops on the wooden signpost. Later on you'll return to this point down the uphill track. When you see Little Loch Ard on your right, drop down through the trees to the water's edge. If you're lucky you might see goldeneye ducks and moorhen near the distant shore.

INFORMATION

Distance: 5 km (3 miles).

Start and finish: Just west of Aberfoyle lies the tiny hamlet of Milton, the township of the mill. It's easy to drive past it, so look out for the restored watermill which has a bright red postbox set into its facing wall. Turn left into the hamlet, drive through it and follow the Forestry Commission signs which take you past an information sign to a large car park.

Terrain: Forest tracks all the way. You can enjoy this walk in ordinary shoes or trainers.

Time: Approximately 1½–2 hours.

Refreshments: Cafés, tea-rooms, restaurants and pubs in Aberfoyle.

Track through forest. Loch Ard is on the right.

An old boat house at the start of this walk.

Return to the track and after 800 m or so you'll reach an obvious bend in the path. Your route goes to the left but before you continue, drop down to the lochside on your right where there a small stretch of peaceful pebble shore – a good spot for a picnic. Watch out for mallard and goldeneye duck.

Return to the track and follow as it bends round to the left and begins to climb steadily upward. After a short distance you'll come across another track veering off to the right, ignore it and continue on the main track. This section of the track is, quite frankly, not terribly interesting as it climbs steadily with dense conifers on either side, but there is a feeling that the increased height will eventually reward you with good views, and it does!

Almost at the high point of the path, when you are beginning to lose hope of any view at all, Ben Lomond comes into view with Loch Ard stretched out in the foreground, resplendent in its wooded setting. It would be nice if the Forestry Commission cut down some of the trees to open up the view a bit, and I dare say in a few years time when these trees are felled down the view will return to its former glory.

Continue on the track, as it bends tightly and then unbends again to rejoin the path followed earlier. Follow your outward route back to the car park.

Climbing high on the forest tracks above Loch Ard.

The House of Milton across the tranquil waters of Loch Ard.

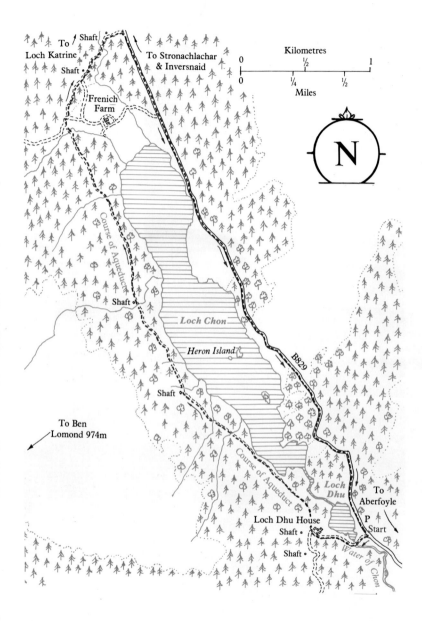

To Loch Katrine

Shaft

Shaft

To Stronachlachar & Inversnaid

Frenich Farm

Kilometres
0   ½   1

0   ¼   ½
Miles

N

Course of Aqueduct

Shaft

Loch Chon

Heron Island

B829

Shaft

To Ben Lomond 974m

Course of Aqueduct

Loch Dhu

To Aberfoyle

Loch Dhu House

Shaft

Shaft

P
Start

Water of Chon

LOCHS DHU AND CHON

As you drive north west on the B829 from Aberfoyle towards Stronachlachar and Inversnaid, you'll pass two lovely tree-fringed lochs, Loch Dhu and Loch Chon ('the black loch' and 'the loch of the dogs'). A pleasant and interesting walk follows the west bank of these lochs and is recommended for those interested in archeological industry, for this route follows the line of an old water aqueduct which runs from Loch Katrine in the north, along the length of Loch Chon, and then southwards to the City of Glasgow.

As you follow this route you'll pass, at frequent intervals, stone pillars, footbridges, lattice domed turrets, pink sandstone watch towers and even a man-made cave, all beautifully constructed in that fine Victorian manner. Made to last! Not surprisingly, the aqueduct is still in use today, over 100 years since it was created.

Leave the car park, walk along the road back towards Aberfoyle and turn right at the path, passing a signpost which indicates 'Waymarked Walking Routes'. Continue past the head of Loch Dhu with lovely views across the loch and over the far woodlands towards the distant hills. Continue past Loch Dhu House and on to a new forestry road.

Until recently there was a lovely footpath which wound its way through the forest all the way along this west shore of Loch Chon. Unfortunately, tree felling has necessitated the building of this new forest road, but your route will use the old footpath as much as possible. After 400m or so on the new road, after a short rise, the old footpath reappears on the left, on top of some grey shale steps. This is a lovely section of the walk, through old oaks, pines and larches.

Soon you'll come across a black iron-plated structure with a turning wheel on top – this is part of the aqueduct which runs from Loch Katrine to Glasgow. As the walk progresses you'll come across more of these aqueduct shafts, built in 1855.

Shortly after this iron-plated building you'll notice

INFORMATION

Distance: 10 km (6 miles).

Start and finish: Car park near the south end of Loch Chon, on B829.

Terrain: Mostly on forest road and good paths which can be wet after rainy weather. A longish road section at the end. Boots are recommended.

Time: Approximately 3–4 hours.

Points of interest: Much of the route follows the line of the Loch Katrine to Glasgow water aqueduct, with some fine examples of Victorian water board architecture. Look out for roe deer, buzzards and some very fine old oak woods. Jays are common in these woods and herons frequent Loch Chon and Loch Dhu.

Refreshments: None.

another structure, a stone building with an iron latticed dome on its top. This is an inspection shaft for the aqueduct, the first of several you will come across. Pass the shaft, cross the footbridge and turn left. Continue following the path, climbing high above the new forestry road before dropping down to meet the road again.

Follow the new road for about 400m; near its end there is a path diversion to the left. At the time of writing this was marked by orange tape tied to the trees. Presumably Forest Enterprise will create proper signposts.

Loch Chon.

Follow the left side of the burn through an area of ancient lichen-covered oak trees, like something out of a Tolkien book. The path soon leads to the second latticed dome. Shortly after comes a long, gently undulating open forest ride, with some fine ancient oaks to remind you what this forest must have been like hundreds of years ago when oak, birch and Scots pine were the dominant trees, when great elks, wolves and bears were the dominant mammals and beavers swam in our lochs and rivers.

After this long and pleasant ride, you'll pass a rocky

crag on the left with a cave in it. The cave is man-
made and actually gives access to the aqueduct. Keep
on, passing through a gap in the wall and pass another
black iron aqueduct on your left. After a further 150
metres, cross a stream by a wooden footbridge, and pass
more green lichen-covered oaks. Pass an old
corrugated iron hut on the right then cross another
stream.

Continue up a short rise and into a dark tunnel
beneath the conifers with little sign of the sky above
you. Pass another lattice domed shaft, over another
stream (with a very fine pool below) and you'll find
yourself on a rather faint track in another fine,
bracken-covered ride. This time some old wooden
marker posts point the way ahead.

This is a lovely section of the walk, following the
meandering path as it weaves its way through the
bracken. I walked this path late on a spring evening
just as daylight was giving way to dusk. Roe deer burst
from the tree cover at the side of the path, stared at me
for a few moments, then ran off into the trees again. In
front of you, you'll see the line of lattice domed shafts
marking the route of the aqueduct over the hill
towards Loch Katrine.

An open view to the right shows up the waters of
Loch Chon beyond Frenich Farm. This lovely stretch
of track continues past another dome, this time
surrounded by an iron railing. Shortly afterwards,
you'll meet a track which leads you up to the B829
road. As you follow this track up to the road, look
behind you. If the weather is clear you'll see an
unexpected and unusual view of the north corrie and
summit cone of Ben Lomond, a particularly fine view
when the hill is snow-covered.

Loch Chon.

Turn right onto the road and follow it back to the car
park. It is possible to leave the road for short sections
where it meets Loch Chon, but much of the lochside
walking is boggy and overgrown. This is a quiet road
and traffic shouldn't prove to be too much of a hazard.
Take great care nevertheless.

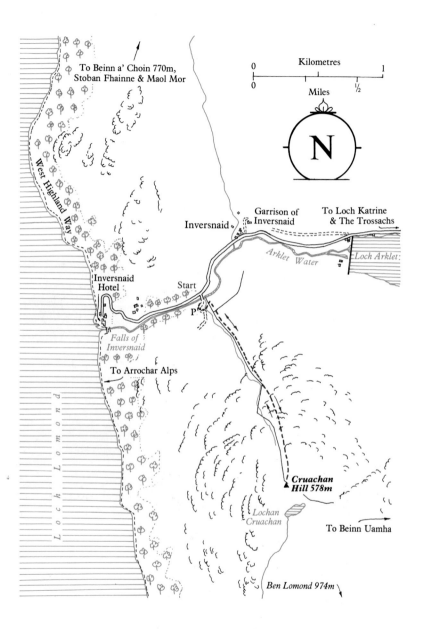

To Beinn a' Choin 770m,
Stoban Fhainne & Maol Mor

0   Kilometres   1

0   Miles   ½

N

West Highland Way

Garrison of
Inversnaid
Inversnaid

To Loch Katrine
& The Trossachs

Arklet Water

Loch Arklet

Inversnaid
Hotel

Start

P

*Falls of
Inversnaid*

To Arrochar Alps

L o c h   L o m o n d

**Cruachan
Hill 578m**

*Lochan
Cruachan*

To Beinn Uamha

Ben Lomond 974m

CRUACHAN HILL

This delightful little hill lies south-west of Loch Arklet on the wild and remote eastern shore of Loch Lomond. Because of the apparent remoteness of this area, there is a real mountaineering quality to the ascent of this hill, even though it's only 578 m/1762 ft in height.

Its ascent offers few difficulties and what it lacks in height it more than compensates for in the splendour of its views. From its summit you can gaze south into the great north corrie of Ben Lomond, the most southerly Munro (mountain over 914 m/3000 ft) in Scotland. Between Cruachan Hill and Ben Lomond lies a wild and untamed corrie, with the steep Cuilness Burn falling through its narrow recesses down towards the Craigrostan shore of Loch Lomond. This is the great hollow that the North of Scotland Hydro Electric Board were keen to flood a number of years ago by pumping water up from Loch Lomond and storing it behind a high 558 m/2000 ft long dam.

Looking down on the site of the old Inversnaid Garrison, from the lower slopes of Cruachan Hill.

INFORMATION

Distance: 5 km (3 miles), with 400 m of ascent.

Start and finish: Take the road from Aberfoyle to Kinlochard and on to Inversnaid. Drive past the head of Loch Arklet, past the Garrison of Inversnaid and the old church which is now used as an outdoor centre. Before dropping steeply down the hill to Inversnaid, a parking place is signposted on the left side of the road. Follow this sign, over a narrow wooden bridge and drive up a winding hill to a fine secluded parking spot, offering good views across the deep trench of Loch Lomond towards the hills known as the Arrochar Alps.

Terrain: Steep heather and grass slopes with some peaty sections. Walking boots are advisable. Also take a compass and the OS 1:50000 Landranger map sheet 56, and know how to use them. Cruachan Hill may be lowly in terms of height, but its situation can attract bad weather.

Refreshments: Hotel at Inversnaid with bar, and tea-room.

Points of interest: The old Garrison fort, although not much can be seen of the original buildings. The West Highland Way runs through the car park of the Inversnaid Hotel below Cruachan Hill, and the Falls of Inversnaid are worth seeing. The summit of the hill is a very fine viewpoint.

Thankfully the plans for this, the biggest pumped storage scheme in Europe, have always been resisted, for this is a high, wild and remote spot, the home of feral goats, red deer and golden eagle. It's best to stay that way.

Cruachan Hill's summit also offers extensive views across the breadth of Loch Lomond to the jumble of high hills, known as the Arrochar Alps, on the far bank: Beinn Vorlich, Ben Vane, Beinn Narnain, the Cobbler and Beinn Ime, as fine a clutch of mountains as you'll find anywhere in the country. Gaze eastwards on a clear day and the whole panorama of the Trossachs lies before you, with Loch Arklet stretching out its long slim finger towards Loch Katrine, running more or less at right angles to it to form a large T-shape of water.

Cruachan Hill across Loch Arklet.

Indeed, as you drive along the road on the north side of Loch Arklet, you'll notice the slopes of Cruachan Hill at the end of the loch, a large corrie giving way to the summit slopes which are connected by a long west-east running ridge to Beinn Uamha (hill of the caves).

The car park was contructed in 1966 by 53 Field Squadron of the Royal Engineers, and a footpath leaves the far left-hand corner by a memorial cairn. Follow this path up through the trees for a short distance and when you reach a deer fence, turn left and cross a burn. There is no path hereabouts and it's quite overgrown. Follow the fence for a short distance to where it runs into another fence. Cross this fence onto the open hillside.

Follow the fence steeply uphill over heathery ground. Go through a gate in another fence and continue uphill. As you plod uphill take a little stop now and again to gaze around you. Behind and below, you'll see the old church and the Garrison, backed by Beinn a' Choin, Stob-an Fhainne and Maol Mor. The Garrison is nowadays a farm but it was originally an 18th century military fort. It was built to try and help control the troublesome Macgregors and indeed, it was Rob Roy Macgregor himself who captured it and destroyed it soon after it was first manned. It was rebuilt and re-garrisoned but burnt down again during the 1745 Jacobite Rising by one of Rob Roy's sons, Seumas Mor ('Big James'). James was acting on the orders of Macgregor of Glen Gyle who was known in Gaelic as Grigor Glun Dubh, or 'Gregor Black-knee' because of a birthmark he had on one of his knees. Grigor was a supporter of Charles Edward Stuart, the Young Pretender.

Cruachan Hill across Loch Arklet.

After its second burning, the garrison was rebuilt again, and was then continually manned until the year 1792 when it was put under the command of a single soldier, a veteran. Sir Walter Scott, in the introduction to his great novel *Rob Roy*, mentions that when he passed the Garrison, 'the venerable warder was reaping his barley crift in all peace and tranquility; and when we asked for admittance to repose ourselves, he told us we would find the key of the Fort under the door.' At one stage in the Garrison's history it was commanded by a certain General Wolfe, who later went on to fame and fortune as a soldier in Quebec, Canada.

After a while the fence takes a sharp bend to the right, but you can continue straight on, over a boggy, peaty section, and then up a steeper section of hill below a crag. The final slopes are fairly steep but don't offer any real problem and the summit cairn is soon reached. Look out for tiny Lochan Cruachan below you. Return the way you came, back down to the car park on the Inversnaid road.

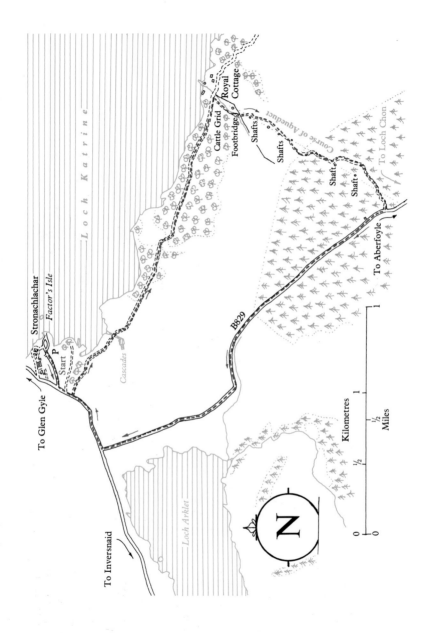

Loch Katrine

Stronachlachar
Factor's Isle
To Glen Gyle
Start
P
Cascades

Cattle Grid
Footbridge
Royal Cottage
Shafts
Shafts
Course of Aqueduct
To Loch Chon
Shaft
Shaft

B829
To Aberfoyle

To Inversnaid
Loch Arklet

N

Kilometres
0   ½   1
0   ½   1
Miles

WATER TO GLASGOW; THE LOCH KATRINE AQUEDUCT

Loch Katrine, as well as being the finest of the Trossachs lochs, is also the main water supply for the City of Glasgow. The loch holds some 14000 million gallons of water at any one time, no doubt due to the average rainfall in the Trossachs of some 2125 mm (85 inches) annually. The quality of the water is extremely high, giving Glasgow the finest supply of any city in the UK.

This walk follows the initial line of that water supply which flows from Loch Katrine to Loch Chon via an underground aqueduct which is marked above ground by a series of towers. This is the beginning of a 42 km journey from Loch Katrine to Glasgow, and the Loch Chon walk in this book follows the line of the aqueduct for several more kilometres.

Work on the aqueduct was started in 1855 in typical Victorian fashion – no expense spared. Even today, the buildings and beautifully manicured grounds around the Water Department's buildings at Stronachlachar are impressive, and it's obvious from the series of towers which trace this underground route that money was never a problem. Bear in mind though that the squads of navvies who built the aqueduct were probably paid no more than subsistence wages. Physical graft came cheap in those days.

INFORMATION

Distance: 7½ km (4½ miles).

Start and finish: Car park at Stronachlachar on Loch Katrine, reached by taking the B829 Inversnaid road from Aberfoyle and turning off as indicated.

Terrain: A nice mixture of easy road, hill track and forest paths, wet and boggy in places. Boots or wellies advised.

Time: Allow about 3 hours.

Refreshments: Nearest refreshments are at the Inversnaid Hotel, or any of the hotels, cafes or restaurants in Aberfoyle. Public toilets in Aberfoyle.

Looking back towards Stronachlachar and the hills of Glen Gyle.

Start at Stronachlachar – a beautifully maintained pier with, in season, the banks of the loch bright with rhododendrons. Go back up the road which leads to the pier on to the main drive. Turn left on to the main drive as though you were going back up to the B829, then take the second road on the left. The road is signposted 'No Unauthorised Vehicles'.

The start of this walk at Stronachlachar.

Walk along the road and enjoy the marvellous views over the banks of pink and violet rhododendrons to the Glen Gyle hills beyond the Factor's Isle. The small island was named after the Duke of Montrose's factor, who was imprisoned there and held to ransom by Rob Roy. The island would have been considerably larger then, as the level of the loch rose markedly when Loch Katrine became a reservoir.

After about 800 m you'll cross some superb cascades which fall down the hill from Loch Arklet, all part of the waterworks system. Although man-made, the cascades are impressive and you may even notice the lone rhododendron bush in the middle of the crashing waters. This particular aqueduct dates from 1895.

You may be walking along a tarmac road, but despite that it's a lovely section of the walk with fine views down the length of the loch to the Glen Gyle hills in the west. From this angle, the high hills appear to choke the upper reaches of the loch. The banks of the loch are nicely wooded hereabouts – oak, rowan and birch predominate.

A cattle grid and gate mark the end of the tarmac section of the road. Beyond the gate is Royal Cottage, the start of the long underground aqueduct which draws the water from Loch Katrine all the way to the City of Glasgow. The cottage is named after a visit from Queen Victoria, who officially opened the aqueduct in 1859.

Just before you reach the cattle grid a rough track leads off to the right. Follow this track uphill as it curves round to the right to join a bubbling stream on the left. Continue on the track, climbing steadily through a pleasant wood of oak and birch. Cross the stream by a little iron footbridge, avoid the track which leads off to the right and climb up to the round stone tower which marks the route of the underground aqueduct which carries the water the 2.42 km to Loch Chon. From this first tower, look uphill to a bizarre assortment of towers and obelisks which mark the route of the aqueduct, and of your walk!

Water cascades from Loch Arklet to Loch Katrine.

Cross the fence and follow the path uphill towards the next tower with the views beginning to open up behind you over Loch Katrine. The path tends to become a little faint hereabouts, but don't worry too much – just follow the towers and obelisks and you won't go wrong.

Soon you'll notice the path veering off to the right towards a flat-topped obelisk as you are halfway up a small hillock. Leave the main path and climb up to the top of the hill for a tremendous viewpoint. Ben Lomond, and its mighty north-east face, rears up in the south. Further right you'll get a glimpse of Loch Arklet in its fold of hills and beyond, the hills of the Arrochar Alps. Behind you, the view extends back to the pink-topped roofs of Stronachlachar and the Balquhidder hills behind.

From the hillock make your way back to the flat-topped obelisk; take care as the path drops steeply down to a ladder stile over the fence. Cross the stile into the forestry plantation and continue following the now obvious path. At the first round tower in the forest, turn left, following a faint path which leads into the trees. Follow this delightful path, eventually running alongside a stream, all the way down to the B829 road.

Turn right on the road and follow it back to Stronachlachar. At the head of Loch Arklet look out for a rowan tree growing out of a large rock – it's split the rock into two jagged parts!

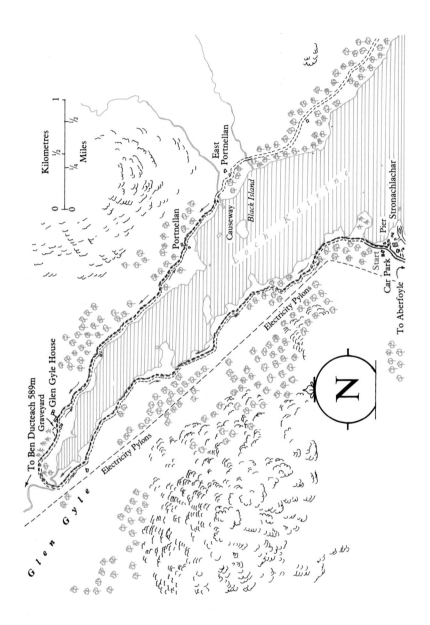

Kilometres

1

½

¼

0

Miles

½

¼

0

Loch Katrine

East Portnellan

Portnellan

Causeway

Black Island

To Ben Ducteach 589m

Graveyard

Glen Gyle House

Electricity Pylons

Electricity Pylons

Glen Gyle

Stronachlachar

Pier

Start

Car Park

To Aberfoyle

N

GLEN GYLE

The waters of Loch Katrine have been harnessed to supply the water needs of the City of Glasgow, but apart from the odd notice telling you not to swim in the reservoir, all is unspoilt and natural once you are away from the eastern end of the loch where the pier, the steamer and the car-park stamps the mark of officialdom.

The western end of the loch, beyond Stronachlachar, is possibly the most delightful part of the Trossachs, and certainly the wildest, but all is not perfect. A line of electricity pylons mar the beauty, a stark reminder of man's spoiling hand. But, such is the scale of this landscape that the pylons are dwarfed, put into a proper perspective by massive mountain slopes, natural woodland and the beauty of the loch itself. This western tip of Loch Katrine, the Glen Gyle shore, is a bit special.

This is, historically, Macgregor territory. On the north shore of Loch Katrine, near its western extremity, is the house of Glengyle where, on 7 March, 1671, a child was born, a son. He was baptised Robert, son of Lt-Col Donald Macgregor, an officer in the army of Charles II, and Margaret Campbell, half-sister to the later despised Campbell of Glenlyon, who was partly responsible for carrying out the evil orders at the Massacre of Glencoe.

Young Robert grew to be one of Scotland's best-loved characters, and even today there is much disagreement as to whether he was a hero, or a villain. Robert, or as he became widely known, Rob Roy ('Roy' coming from the Gaelic 'ruadh' meaning red, after his hair), became chief of the clan on his father's death in 1693. In fact he wasn't next in line of descent for the title, being only the second son, but such was his personality and influence over his elder brother John, even at the young age of 22, that his brother declined the responsibilities in favour of Rob.

History records Rob Roy as not being very tall, but his broad stocky build, and strong personal charisma, stood him head and shoulders above others in any social gathering. It is said that his mood could change

INFORMATION

Distance: 16 km (10 miles) there and back.

Start and finish: Stronachlachar car park on Loch Katrine, reached by taking the B729 road from Aberfoyle to Inversnaid and turning off as indicated.

Time: Allow 4 hours.

Terrain: Tarmac road all the way. This is also a lovely route for a bicycle.

Refreshments: None. Nearest hotel is Inversnaid on Loch Lomondside.

Looking west towards the head of Glen Gyle.

from cold anger to uproarious laughter at the drop of a hat, and he had a devilish sense of humour, greatly enjoying practical jokes and in particular, putting one over on authority!

He had vowed to help the downtrodden, and in those wild days, protection like that required a strong show of muscle and arms. He also inherited from his father the captaincy of the Highland Watch. This was a type of semi-official blackmail business – in those days of widespread cattle reiving, bands of men protected the cattle of the rich merchants and farmers who lived on the borders of the Highland Line, in return for an annual fee. This protection racket became big business, and was even later approved by the Government, no doubt delighted to see the rebel clans settle down as prosperous businessmen.

These watches, as they became known, were set up throughout the Highlands and Rob Roy's father became joint Captain of the Highland Watch. In time, the members of the various watches took a high social position in the clan set-up – they were in the privileged position of being allowed to carry arms, and could exercise some authority over their neighbours. This authority was often flouted, and a great amount of cattle stealing, or lifting, went on as well, under the respectable and approved mask of the Highland Watch. Rob Roy ran his Watch in a shrewd business-like manner, and woe betide anyone who was late with his dues, whether he was the local minister, or the Lord Justice Clerk. Rob Roy was no great respecter of rank.

The walk around the head of Loch Katrine, past the house of Glen Gyle and down the lochside to the old ancient burial place of the Macgregors at Portnellan is all on tarmac road, but don't let that put you off. You are extremely unlikely to come across any motor vehicle, and if you do it will be a Water Board vehicle or a Landrover from the estate.

Glen Gyle House at the head of Loch Katrine.

From the car park, go back up to the main drive and turn right into the road which says 'No Unauthorised Vehicles'. Go through the white gate at the side and follow the road, past the houses and on round the shores of Loch Katrine. Soon, across the waters of the loch, you'll see the two small buildings of Portnellan and along the shore to their right, the strange little causeway that was built to recreate the ancient burial place of some of the Clan Macgregor – but more of that later.

The road continues on its meandering way amid superlative scenery, marred only by the marching line of electricity pylons which goose-step their way up the length of Glen Gyle. This supply comes all the way from the Ben Cruachan hydro-electric scheme at Loch Awe.

Carry on along the road and soon the white house of Glen Gyle will come into view – the birthplace of Rob Roy himself. In Rob's day the scene would have been very different. The waters of the loch wouldn't have been so high, the present high level of flooding being due to the reservoir. Instead of water as it is now, the front of Glengyle House would have been broad fields, where black kye, the small highland cattle, would probably have grazed. Glengyle, on an ancient drove road between the glens of the west and the cattle trysts at Stirling and Falkirk, would have been a regular halt for the drovers as they took their herds along the very route you are now walking.

Carry on round the head of the loch and note the waterfall high above Glengyle House. Just before you reach the house a little path enters the trees and leads to a small private graveyard, the final resting place of the Glen Gyle Macgregors. A nephew of Rob Roy, Gregor Macgregor, who was known as 'Black Knee' Macgregor because of a large birthmark on his leg, is buried here and you can see his gravestone. Gregor was reputed to have been 'out' with Bonnie Prince Charlie in 1745.

Continue past the house, with some fine views back up Glen Gyle to Ben Ducteach. Pass the cottages at Portnellan and continue onwards for 800 m or so where a steep grassy slope on your right leads down to a man-made causeway which holds some very old gravestones. When Loch Katrine was made into a reservoir, the natural level of the loch had to be raised. Since the new level threatened to drown an ancient Macgregor burial site, this causeway was built and the old gravestones moved on to it. The original graveyard is a good three metres below the water.

An older grave in the Glen Gyle House graveyard depicting the old Macgregor motif.

Return to Stronachlachar the way you came.

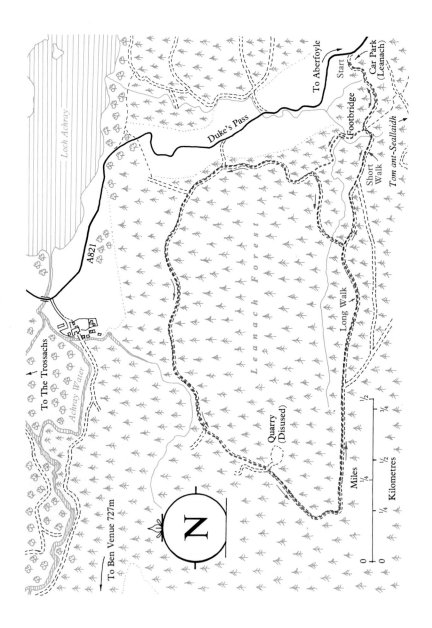

LEANACH FOREST

This is a short walk on the heavily forested eastern slopes of Ben Venue. While the distance is not great, and the mass coniferisation would normally discourage you from walking in an area like this, there is a stretch of natural woodland within the forest which is well worth visiting.

It's said that Sir Walter Scott loved walking on these slopes, long before the introduction of conifers, when birch and oak reigned supreme. At the end of the 19th century there was a great deal of local concern when the natural deciduous woods were cut down, and it was the Forestry Commission, during the Second World War, who began the replanting, using prisoners of war, and trees from North America, Japan and Scandinavia.

INFORMATION

Distance: About 4 km (2½ miles).

Start and finish: Forestry Commission car park at Leanach, just off the Duke's Pass road (A821) near the viewpoint of Tom an t-Seallaidh.

Terrain: Forest tracks and narrow undulating footpath which can be wet. Boots or wellies advised in bad weather.

Time: Give yourself about 1½ hours; the old section of footpath is a good place to linger.

Refreshments: There is a tea-room at the pier at the Trossachs, and cafes and tea-rooms in Aberfoyle. The David Marshall Lodge also serves tea, coffee and soft drinks and offers a wealth of information about Queen Elizabeth Forest Park.

Leaving the forest road to re-enter the woods on an ancient through-route from Aberfoyle to the Trossachs.

The view from the car park itself makes it a worthwhile stop, from the bulk of Ben Venue in the west, the slopes tumbling down in rocky bluffs to the Trossachs itself, where little Ben A'n raises its head in some wonder, as though surprised to be amongst such grand company.

Two walks start from this car park, a short circuit marked by gold rings on the marker posts, and a longer walk, marked by silver rings. The longer route has little justification, other than the fact that it offers a long walk-in to Ben Venue and that there is a backpackers' campsite halfway round its circuit; the Harry Lawrie Camp Site, named after a police sergeant from Killin who was also leader of the Killin Mountain Rescue Team. He was killed in a helicopter accident on Ben More near Crianlarich during a rescue operation a number of years ago.

Overnight emergency shelter.

The camp site also boasts a rather interesting 'bothy'; built entirely of timber, this 'tepee' style of shelter is the invention of a young designer, Charles Gulland, who created several such shelters in various places throughout the country with encouragement from the then Countryside Commission for Scotland.

Head into the forest from the car park, follow the obvious forestry road and after 400 m look out for a marker post on your right; it indicates a narrow and rather overgrown footpath which leads into the forest itself. Cross over some fallen trees and enjoy this little winding path as it descends through lovely overgrown birch and larch woods.

Reach an obvious grassy ride, cross it, and re-enter the trees where you'll find a small wooden footbridge crossing a shallow stream. This almost forgotten footpath follows the line of an ancient trail which once took travellers from Aberfoyle to the Trossachs, long before the advent of the Duke's Pass or any other motorable road. It was probably walked by Sir Walter Scott, and most certainly would have been used by clansmen returning to their highland glens from forays into the lowlands.

Cross the footbridge and continue through the woods. You'll notice many more conifers now, thickening the canopy overhead, and with the sunlight filtering through the branches above the atmosphere can become quite surreal – almost eerie!

There are many fallen trees in this section; victims of the storms of the past few winters. Try to imagine what it would have been like to have been here at the height of such a storm, with the thunder cracking overhead, the wind roaring through the treetops and the trees themselves creaking and groaning and swaying as if they were in pain. Those lying all around you were the casualties of those storms.

Make your way over, or if easier, under, the fallen corpses – sorry, I mean trees – and re-find the traces of the footpath, which now leads off to the right and climbs a small bank, before merging with the main forest road. Turn left at the marker sign, and follow the road.

At the first junction, turn left, still on the forest road, and continue on this road all the way back to the car park.

View of the Trossachs from the starting point of this walk.

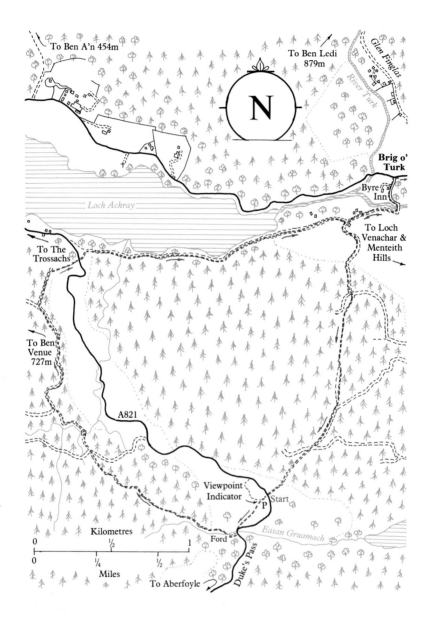

To Ben A'n 454m

To Ben Ledi
879m

N

River Turk

Glen Finglas

Brig o'
Turk

Byre
Inn

To Loch
Venachar &
Menteith
Hills

Loch Achray

To The
Trossachs

To Ben
Venue
727m

A821

Viewpoint
Indicator

P Start

Easan Gruamach

Kilometres

Ford

0   ½   1

0   ¼   ½

Miles

Duke's Pass

To Aberfoyle

BRIG O'TURK

INFORMATION

Distance: 10 km (6 miles).

Start and finish: Park at the signposted viewpoint on the Trossachs side of the Duke's Pass (A821).

Terrain: Forest tracks and footpaths, many of which tend to be quite wet and boggy at times. Wellies or walking boots recommended.

Time: Allow 3 hours.

Refreshments: The Byre Inn, near Brig o'Turk, is a good spot for a halfway drink or coffee. There is a tea-room in Brig o'Turk.

Close to the very heart of the Trossachs area, the tiny hamlet of Brig o'Turk lies in a lovely setting of forest, loch and mountain. It is at the foot of Glen Finglas, once an important cattle droving trail and between Loch Achray and Loch Vennachar. To its south lies the huge Queen Elizabeth Forest Park, and this walk takes you through some of the older parts of this forest, starting and finishing at a wonderful viewpoint which portrays the Trossachs in all its mountainous glory. Halfway through the walk you visit Brig o'Turk itself, its name derived from the word *tuirc* – Gaelic for 'wild boar'.

An indicator points out the various features to be seen from the car park, from Ben Venue to Loch Katrine with the Glen Gyle hills beyond, shapely Ben A'n, Glen Kinglas and Ben Vane, the back of Ben Ledi and Lochs Vennachar and Drunkie with the Menteith Hills beyond – a wonderful panorama.

Leave the view indicator and head due south, along a rocky path patched up here and there with old railway sleepers, then through scrub birch and bracken. Follow this faint footpath until it reaches another path. Turn right onto this new path and follow it as it drops down very steeply to the roadside at the bridge over the Easan Gruamach – the grumbling burn!

The direction indicator at the start of the walk, looking over the Trossachs.

Cross the bridge and immediately turn right, back into the woods on a narrow and faint path. Follow this up the left bank of the burn and in a short distance cross over the burn, go through a broken gate, and into a conifer plantation. Follow the path as it winds its way through the woods. It's mostly quite clear but here and there you have to duck below some low hanging branches to make your way through.

The old farm near Brig o'Turk.

After 15 minutes or so you'll come to another forestry track. Cross it and follow the marked footpath into the trees again. (This path is part of an old route which ran from Aberfoyle to the Trossachs, as mentioned in the Leanach Walk, a trail once greatly enjoyed by Sir Walter Scott.) Go through the woods until you reach another forestry track, then go right. Follow this track mostly downhill, with views of pointed Ben A'n opening up above the trees in front of you.

Soon you'll pass an access road coming in from the right; 200–300 m beyond that, turn right on to a narrower and less frequented forest track. Just before the end of this track, about 150 m along its length, turn right on to a faint footpath through the trees. Follow this down to the road, through an area of bog myrtle, bracken and birch.

Cross the main road and follow the footpath down towards Loch Achray. This path soon joins a wider hard-surfaced track. Turn right on to this track and within a couple of hundred metres it joins the Achray

Forest Drive road. Turn left and follow it, through a small plantation, and on to open moor again. Ahead of you lie some old farm buildings, beyond a fence. Cross the fence by the stile, pass the farm buildings, and continue on this track until you reach an old stone footbridge which crosses the Achray Water. Go over the bridge, past a house on the right, go through another gate and you'll find a delightful little pub, the Byre Inn, on your left. This is a lovely spot for a short break.

To visit Brig o'Turk itself turn right on to the main road and follow it into the village.

Ben A'n from the south shore of Loch Achry.

From the Byre Inn, return to the old farm buildings adjacent to the Achray Forest Drive, cross the stile onto the drive, and turn left. Follow the broad driveway over a hill and just before you enter the forest, look to your left for a view of Loch Vennachar seen 'head-on' in the distance below the Menteith Hills.

A couple of hundred metres further on you'll reach a 'Y' junction. It's time to leave the broad forest track, so continue straight on, turning neither left nor right, by a narrow footpath below a large prominent oak tree.

Keep following the footpath down through birch and oaks to another forest road. Cross over this road, then immediately over a small burn and climb the hillside in front of you, staying on the narrow footpath. The path climbs gently and pleasantly through some birch trees before swinging into an obvious bracken-covered forest ride with conifers on either side. Follow this ride, especially if you lose the footpath, which becomes indistinct here and there because of fallen trees.

Climb steadily out of the ride and on to a forest road. Go right and follow it until it abuts on to another forest track. Cross this new track and find the narrow footpath which climbs the hill opposite. It may well be covered with bracken. Head slightly to your right, making for the obvious firebreak in the trees ahead of you. The path soon becomes clear again and climbs steadily, eventually crossing the Duke's Pass road where another footpath leads up to the Forest Park view indicator.

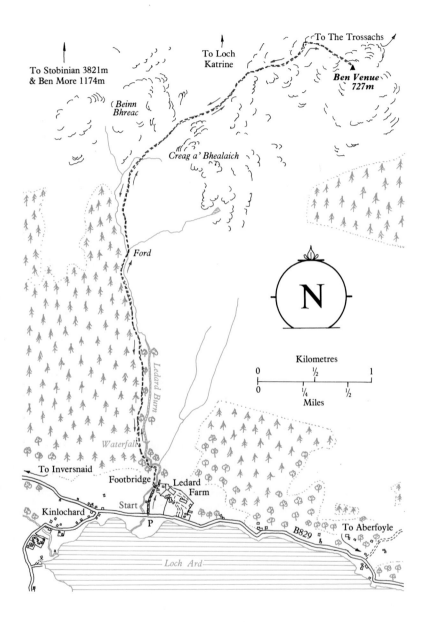

To Stobinian 3821m
& Ben More 1174m

To Loch
Katrine

To The Trossachs

*Beinn
Bhreac*

Ben Venue
727m

Creag a' Bhealaich

Ford

Ledard Burn

N

Kilometres

0   ½   1

0   ¼   ½

Miles

Waterfall

To Inversnaid

Footbridge

Ledard
Farm

Start

Kinlochard

P

B829

To Aberfoyle

Loch Ard

BEN VENUE

Ben Venue, the Hill of the Caves, is one of the finest 'wee hills' in the southern highlands. With its twin tops, its western outliers, and its rugged countenance, it towers over the craggy landscape of the Trossachs, and yet is an easy enough hill to climb. The slopes which tumble down towards the shores of Loch Katrine contain the Bealach nan Bo, the Pass of the Cattle, a legendary if possibly mythical trade route in centuries past for stolen cattle being brought back from the lowlands to the Macgregor lands at the west of Loch Katrine.

Close by is Coire nan Urisgean, or the 'Corrie of the Goblins'. Sir Walter Scott, who roamed this area and found inspiration for his works, depicted the Goblin's Corrie as a retreat for Ellen Douglas and her father after they had withdrawn from Roderick Dhu's stronghold on Eilean Molach.

INFORMATION

Distance: 13 km (8 miles), with 400 m of ascent.

Start and finish: Car park at Ledard Farm on the B829 Aberfoyle to Inversnaid road.

Terrain: This is a serious mountain walk with some steep slopes, muddy conditions, and the route can often be covered in mist. Walkers should be familiar with map and compass techniques and should carry waterproofs, gloves, warm hat, plenty of food and a hot drink.

Map: Walkers should carry the OS 1:50000 Landranger map sheet 56.

Refreshments: Hotels, cafés, restaurants and public toilets in Aberfoyle.

On the summit ridge with Lochs Achray and Vennachar stretching into the distance.

Rather than tackle the hill head-on, up and over its steep and craggy bluffs from the Loch Katrine side, this walk starts from Ledard. From the roadside a footpath sign points the way, proclaiming that it is 7 miles (11 km) to the Trossachs via the summit of Ben Venue.

Take the track which leads past the farm, well known for its breeding of Cashmere goats, and stop for a moment at a fine pool and waterfall just behind the farm. Sir Walter Scott stayed here while working on his notes for *Rob Roy* and *Waverley* and apparently sat and worked beside the pool when the weather was good.

Near the summit, looking out over Loch Katrine towards the Crianlarich hills.

Cross the footbridge over the Ledard Burn and follow the obvious path northwards. In its lower stretches it is *extremely* boggy, but it does improve considerably as you climb higher. Follow this track as it climbs northwards, eventually carrying you high onto the eastern slopes of one of Venue's outliers, Beinn Bhreac. Here, a wide bealach takes you on to the craggy slopes of Ben Venue itself. Even at this point, the first real views of the day to the north-west begin to impress.

Away to the west, Loch Katrine stretches itself out, one of its ancient arms cut off by the strip of land at Stronachlachar. That old arm is now Loch Arklet, running in a transverse line towards the deep trench which holds Loch Lomond. To the north the Crianlarich hills bow their heads to the higher tops of

On the summit ridge.

Stobinian and Ben More and further east the Ben Lawers range all but dwarfs the neighbouring Tarmachans beyond the tops of Stuc a' Chroin and Ben Vorlich.

Continue over the high bealach between Beinn Bhreac and Creag a' Bhealaich and continue along the ridge in a north-easterly direction towards the summit ridge of Ben Venue. The footpath becomes steeper now and weaves its way through some rocky outcrops to lead up to the first of Ben Venue's two summits. Enjoy the view from here, across Loch Katrine to the Loch Lomond hills and the peaks of the Arrochar Alps.

Return to the path and follow it as it wends its way through the summit outcrops and shortly after, reaches the summit itself. Ahead of you the view opens up eastwards, out along the silvery lengths of Loch Achray and Loch Vennachar towards Ben Ledi and the Menteith Hills. The view from the summit trig pillar is extensive, and almost belies Ben Venue's original name. In an old Statistical Account, the hill is recorded as A'Bheinn Mheanbh, *the small peak*.

Although you can descend to the north, down to the Trossachs, I wouldn't recommend it for the purposes of this book. It is steep, rocky, and is often slippery, and it is much safer to return the way you came, back to the bealach between Beinn Bhreac and Creag a' Bhealaich, and then by the footpath back to Ledard Farm.

Loch Katrine and the snow-covered Crianlarich hills.

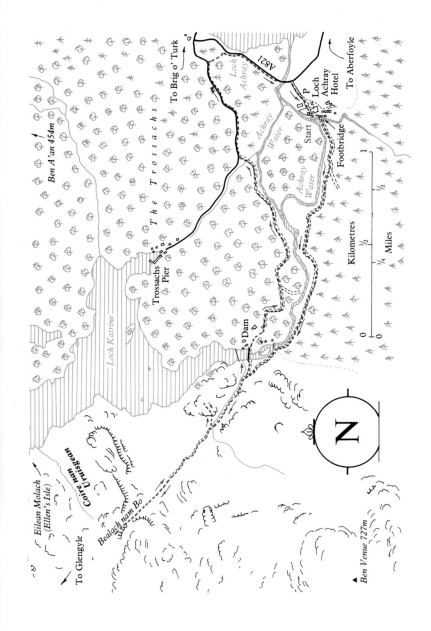

THE CORRIE OF THE GOBLINS

This walk takes you into the very heartland of the Trossachs, to that jumble of wooded crags and rocky bluffs at the eastern end of Loch Katrine. Sir Walter Scott described the spot well when he wrote;

> So wondrous wild the whole might seem,
> The scenery of a faery dream.

But it's goblins, not faeries, which are the subject of this walk. On the south shore of Loch Katrine, an ancient pass slices through the hillside between the summit of Ben Venue and the loch. This is the Bealach nan Bo, where reputedly the Macgregor reivers drove their stolen cattle en route to Glengyle at the head of Loch Katrine. Below the Bealach, to the west, is a corrie called Coire nan Uruisgean, the 'Corrie of the Urisks, or Goblins'. This was reputedly the meeting place for all the goblins in Scotland, who gathered here to plan and plot amid the deep heather and boulder-scarred hollows.

These urisks, explains Dr Graham in his *Scenery of the Southern Confines of Perthshire*, published in 1806, 'were a sort of lubbery supernatural, who could be gained over by kind attention to perform the drudgery of a farm. They were supposed to be spread throughout the highlands each in his own wild recess, but the solemn meetings of the order were regularly held in the cave of Benvenew.'

If all this sounds rather unlikely it's important to remember that we don't have to go back far into our history to recall a time when the people of highland Scotland were extremely superstitious and had a vivid belief in the supernatural. Even today, there are people living in Scotland who have, at least, an open mind about such things. This whole Trossachs area must have had a supernatural reputation at one time for according to the eminent Gaelic scholar, Professor W. J. Watson, the name Loch Katrine is derived from Loch *Ceiteirein*, the 'Loch of the Furies or Fiends'. Professor Watson also recalled that an old man who lived in nearby Brig o' Turk, Parlan MacFarlane, once

INFORMATION

Distance: 8 km (5 miles).

Start and finish: Car park at Loch Achray Hotel, on A821.

Terrain: Forestry track, muddy footpaths, and some steeper rockier footpath. Good boots or wellies recommended.

Time: Allow yourself about 3–3½ hours for the return trip. Longer if you visit the Trossachs pier and tea-rooms.

Toilets: At the Trossachs pier.

Refreshments: There is a tea-room at the Trossachs pier, and tea, coffee, meals and drinks can be obtained in the Loch Achray Hotel.

told him that, 'There is a water-bull on Loch Katrine: I myself have not seen the bull, but I have seen the calf!'

The walk begins from the Loch Achray Hotel. Walk round to the back of the hotel, cross a footbridge over the river and head uphill on a forestry road passing a sign which points the way to Ben Venue and the Bealach nan Bo. Continue on this path, with increasingly good views of the rocky bluffs of Ben Venue ahead of you.

At the bisection of paths go right; continue on this track with the Achray Water on your right. Now and again, through the trees on your right, you'll catch some glimpses of rocky Ben A'an.

This is a lovely stretch of track – Forestry Commission footpath walking at its best. The trees aren't claustrophobically close together, but well spaced out, offering marvellous views of the wooded crags and knolls of Ben Venue. Once again, Sir Walter Scott caught the atmosphere of the area when he wrote,

> High in the south huge Ben Venue,
> Down on the lake in masses threw,
> Crags, knolls, and mounds confusedly hurled,
> The fragments of an earlier world.

It's on this stretch of track that you'll catch your first glimpse of the notch in the skyline that is the Bealach nan Bo, the Pass of the Cattle. Local tradition has it that Rob Roy Macgregor used this route to drive his stolen cattle back to his home at Glengyle, at the western end of Loch Katrine. There was a drove road along the south shore of Loch Katrine, but it seems unlikely that any drover would take his beasts over such a precipitous route when there was a perfectly good drove road just a short distance away. It's a nice story though, and fits the character of Rob Roy. By such stuff are romantic writers made!

At the end of the forest track cross a ladder stile, and continue on the footpath straight ahead with the fence on your right. Pass the dam on your right (you'll return to this point later) and continue straight on.

The path now climbs over quite a muddy section, but it doesn't last too long. Follow the path to a metal gate which has a ladder stile immediately beside it. Cross the stile and follow the path to the left. You will return to this point shortly, but for the moment you want to continue through a very pleasant corrie to the climb up to the notch of the Bealach nan Bo.

About 300 m beyond the metal gate you'll pass an obvious holly tree beside the stream on your right, and 100 m beyond that the path crosses the burn and continues through a wide and very pleasant bracken-covered corrie to the steeper climb up to the Bealach nan Bo itself. On the other side of the bealach lies the rock-strewn Coire nan Uruisgean, the Corrie of the Goblins!

Once you've scoured the area for goblins, return the way you came, back down across the bracken-covered corrie to where the footpath crosses the burn again. On your left is a prominent heathery knoll, and it's worth climbing it for the view down to Loch Katrine and Ellen's Isle. This little island was immortalised by Scott as the home of Ellen Douglas, heroine of *The Lady of the Lake*. The proper name of the island is Eilean Molach.

Return to the burn, cross it and follow the path back to the metal gate. Cross the stile and follow the original route for about 60 m to the end of the fence which lies on your left. Leave the original path here and turn left at the end of the fence, following a faint track through the birches around a rocky outcrop. It feels quite steep and precipitous, but soon some steps appear which take you down quite safely to the dam at the end of the loch.

Cross the dam and go right, past the house. You're back on tarmac road now, so look out for cars. Follow this minor road to the main road which runs to the Trossachs pier. You can either go left to the pier itself where there are toilets and a tea-room, or turn right to return to your starting point. Take great care walking along this stretch of road, for it can become very busy, especially at weekends and holidays. At a prominent left turn in the road, a footpath leads off through the trees on the right. Follow it as it takes you nicely across to a picnic area just a few hundred metres from the Loch Achray Hotel.

The foot of
Loch Katrine.

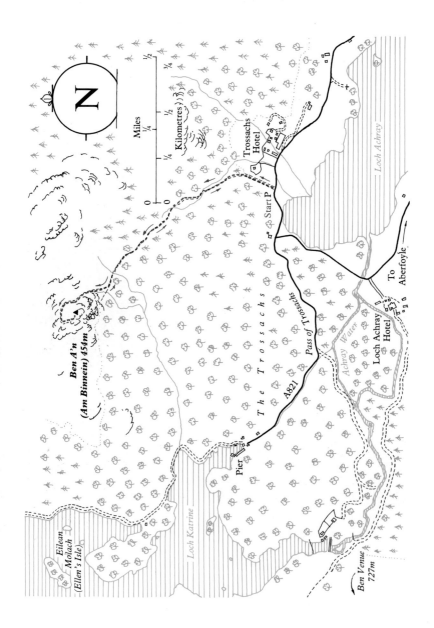

LITTLE BEN A'N

The old name of this fine little peak is Am Binnein, the Rocky Peak, but it was changed by Sir Walter Scott to Ben A'n and so it has stayed. Drive over the Duke's Pass from Aberfoyle to the Trossachs and ahead of you a long line of hills approach from the east and at their western end, standing up like an afterthought, is the shapely peak of this lovely little mountain.

I've called this walk 'Little Ben A'n', but the height of the hill, 454 m/1520 ft is out of all proportion to its character, which is immense. Not only is it a pleasant afternoon stroll for those who don't mind a steep climb, but the hill's south-facing rocky flanks are also enjoyed by rock climbers, with a myriad of good routes of all grades.

INFORMATION

Distance: 6 km (4 miles) with 400 m of ascent.

Start and finish: Forestry Commission car park on A821 on the north shore of Loch Achray, close to the turreted grandeur of the newly refurbished Trossachs Hotel.

Terrain: Steep forest paths and steep and rocky mountain path, often running with water. Good boots are advised.

Time: Allow yourself at least 3–4 hours to really enjoy a relaxed ascent with plenty of time to enjoy the views.

Refreshments: There are two hotels within walking distance of the foot of Ben A'n, the Trossachs Hotel and the Achray Hotel, and a tea-room and public toilets at the Trossachs pier.

Scrambling on the summit rocks with Loch Katrine stretched out behind.

Cross the road from the car park and follow the signpost. This initial section of path is steep and can be muddy but it does allow you to gain height quickly and directly. Take your time here – this isn't a long walk and there's no point in exhausting yourself at this early stage. Enjoy the birdsong and the views opening behind you as you climb up below the canopy of pines.

Ben A'n from the top of the forest.

After a while the steepness relents considerably, and a signpost indicates a viewpoint to the left. It's worthwhile leaving the path and visiting this viewpoint as it offers your first glimpse of the day of your destination, Ben A'n. It's a good view too – framed by spruce and larch, the peak looks steep and exposed and for all the world like a mountain several times its height.

Return to the path and continue uphill. Soon you'll leave the trees behind and the views begin to open up – across to the crags, bluffs and corries of Ben Venue and the long stretch of Loch Katrine, the finest of all the Trossachs lochs. In August and early September the heather of these slopes blooms in brilliant exuberance and contrasts vividly with the greenery of the trees. Later on the grasses turn blond and the leaves lighten into yellows and ochres, reds and russets, a time of year when the Trossachs are at their most splendid.

Continue on the path and begin to climb again, up wet and broken ground, helped significantly by some

Ben A'n from the south
shore of Loch Achray.

sensible path construction work. Higher up this section of path there is a lot of loose rock and scree and after heavy rain there is always a lot of running water. Climb up over the this rough ground, contour round the back of the hill, cross some wet, mossy areas, and then climb up the final few metres to the rocky summit.

And what a summit this is – a fine rocky eyrie with magnificent views towards the west and the north-west. On clear days all the Arrochar hills are clearly seen, from the unmistakable outline of the Cobbler to Ben Vorlich. Further to the right the Crianlarich hills come into view, with the twin summits of Ben More and Stobinian particularly imposing. Loch Katrine stretches impressively into the heartland of MacGregor country, and across the waters below you lies the ancient pass of the Bealach nan Bo at the foot of Ben Venue.

Take time to enjoy this summit, and if you enjoy a challenge try to sprint up the Ten Second Slab. This is the rocky boiler-plate slab which leans up to the summit cairn, and it's claimed that good climbers will scale it in 10 seconds. Ordinary walkers will probably take just a tad longer!

There is a descent route from Ben A'n which leads off to the north and west and which goes down through the forest to the north shore of Loch Katrine, but it is an ill-defined and awkward path, often very wet and slippery. Best advice is to return to the car park the way you came.

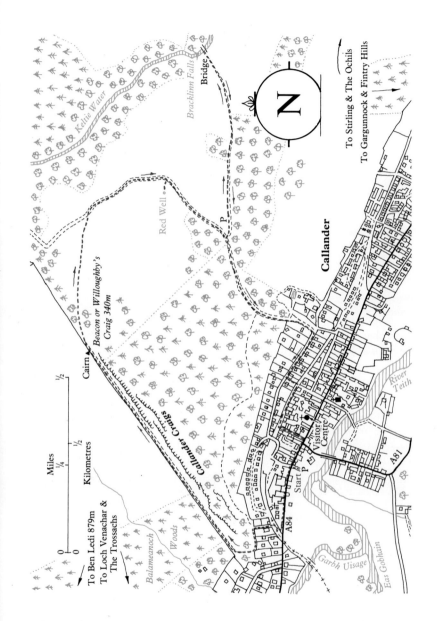

To Stirling & The Ochils
To Gargunnock & Fintry Hills

N

Bridge

Bracklinn Falls

Keltie Water

Red Well

P

Callander

River Teith

A81

Visitor Centre

Start
P

A84

Garbh Uisage

Eas Gobhuin

Beacon or Willoughby's
Craig 340m

Cairn

Callander Craigs

Balameanoch Woods

Miles
¼   ½
Kilometres
¼   ½
0
0

To Ben Ledi 879m
To Loch Venachar &
The Trossachs

CALLANDER CRAIGS

The Callander Craigs, or the Callander Crag walk, has been a popular route with locals and visitors to this highland border town for generations. To the north-east of the town, the hill rises abruptly and steeply on its wooded slopes, with its bare crags visible through the highest trees.

The highest point of the Craigs, Beacon Craig or as it is locally known, Willoughby's Craig, rises to a height of 340 m. Its ascent, while steep and rough in places despite the Forestry Commission's attempt to create a path all the way to the summit, is not too difficult, although there are one or two points near the summit where youngsters should be warned not to stray too close to the edge.

From the car park, turn left onto the main street, walk along it for a short distance and turn right into Tulipan Crescent just before you reach the Tulipan Lodge Guest House. Turn left after the last house in the crescent at the signpost which says, 'To the Crags and Woodland Walk'.

Take the obvious path uphill into the trees where you'll find a Stirling District Council notice board outlining the walks available. Follow the footpath leftwards after the noticeboard, through some very fine woods. These really are magnificent woodlands, with oaks, chestnuts, beeches and firs mixing with the younger conifers.

The path climbs gently at first, below the wide green canopy, and then more steeply up a series of wooden steps. Take great care on these steps, especially on the descents, as the timber frame becomes very slippery when wet. Most footpath building agencies avoid building staircases like this nowadays, as the steps break up the natural rhythm of walking and many walkers tend to disregard them, creating an eroded pathway up the side of the steps instead.

Soon the path begins to zigzag up some steeper sections, and some of the wooden steps seem to be nearly a metre in height! About halfway up the hill, just beside a huge double-trunked beech tree, another

INFORMATION

Distance: 7 km (4½ miles), with 300 m ascent.

Start and finish: Park in the car park on the south side of the main street, opposite the Dreadnought Hotel.

Terrain: Some steep climbing initially and some exposed drops near the top of the Craigs. Take particular care on the wooden steps as you ascend the Craigs and near the Bracklinn Falls. They become particularly slippery in damp weather. Good walking boots are advised.

Points of Interest: The widespread view from the top of the Craigs, the Red Well and the Bracklinn Falls.

Refreshments: Hotels, cafés and restaurants in Callander.

The Red Well.

path leads off to the right to the first viewpoint over the town. It is a fine view, but is best in winter when the trees are devoid of leaves.

Make your way back on to the main path and follow it up another series of steps. Continue following the footpath uphill; near the top of the hill the path becomes a bit rougher and rockier, but take your time, take care, and you won't experience any great difficulty.

The top section of the walk is extremely pleasant, and the path becomes less steep as it winds its way through young birches and pines. Here and there a break in the trees allow you views out over the town of Callander towards the distant Gargunnock and Fintry Hills. But these views are nothing compared to the panorama which opens up as you reach the summit cairn, the Beacon Craig or Willoughby's Craig. Look westwards along the length of silvery Loch Vennachar, its head seemingly choked by the high hills of the Trossachs. To the right you look into the very bosom of Ben Ledi, that great wild north-east corrie, and eastwards your gaze carries you along the broad strath to Stirling, the Ochils and beyond to the dim outline of the Pentlands south of Edinburgh.

Leave the cairn, built in 1887 to commemorate Queen Victoria's Silver Jubilee, and enjoy the lovely descent path through young birch, Scots pine and good views over the open moorland. As you descend the final few metres to the road, the path winds its way through some dense scrub birch. Here and there it's a bit tricky to follow, and watch out for slippery roots and boulders.

You'll soon reach the road; turn right and follow it back towards the town. After a while you'll come across an old faded signpost on your right, which points out a footpath which leads to the Red Well, a mineral spring, about 50–60m off the road. This is a semi-circular stone built wall with a central plaque embedded in a large stone. Below it a pipe supplies the red ore-coloured water. The plaque contains the message:

THE RED WELL (*Chalybeate Spring*) OF OLD TIME
REPUTE RESTORED BY CALLANDER AMENITY
COMMITTEE APRIL 1924

Return to the road and continue the descent as far as a car park on your left which gives access to a footpath which runs to the Bracklinn Falls, where according to old legend, Sir Walter Scott rode his horse over a rickety bridge for a wager. Follow the path for about 800 m until you reach a kissing gate which gives access to a flight of wooden steps which lead down to the falls. A large rock protects the bridge which makes a good viewing platform. This is not the rickety bridge of Sir Walter Scott's day, but a firm iron one.

It's a grand spot, with the River Keltie tumbling over a a succession of huge sandstone blocks which form a rough, and gigantic, natural staircase. The colouring is rich, with a profusion of mountain ash, oak and beech. Sir Walter Scott, never one to miss a good scene, brought the Bracklinn Falls into his great story, *The Lady of the Lake*:

The Bracklinn Falls.

> As Bracklinn's chasm, so black and steep,
> Receives her roaring linn,
> As the dark caverns of the deep,
> Suck the wild whirlpool in,
> So did the deep and darksome pass,
> Devour the battle's mingled mass.

It's a good description, and none too exaggerated either.

After you've soaked in the atmosphere of the falls, make your way back to the car park and the road which descends into Callander. Follow the road downhill, ignoring all the signs which indicate paths going off on various woodland walks to your right. About a kilometre from the Bracklinn Falls car park you'll reach the rear of a house, Arden House, which has a footpath running down the left of its garden wall. Follow this path past the house, and then past another house, and it will bring you out on Ancaster Road. Turn right, and make your way back into the town, taking any one of a number of narrow lanes which turn left from Ancaster Road down to the Main Street.

The town of Callander.

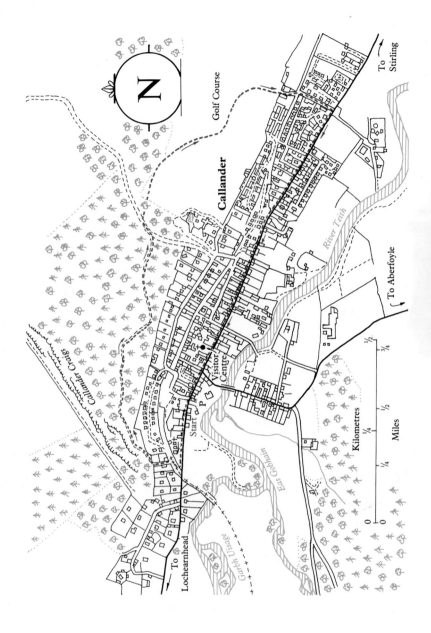

CALLANDER TOWN WALK I

There are a handful of towns in Scotland which boast the nickname 'Gateway to the Highlands'. Callander's claim is more than justified. This fine town, beautifully situated at the junction of the River Teith with the Leny, has long been popular as a tourist resort and indeed as a centre for exploring the hills and lochs of the southern Highlands. Indeed it's been claimed that Callander has, in proportion to its population, the largest number of hotels and guest houses of any town in Scotland. In the 1960s it received much prominence as the town where the original series of the popular television programme, *Dr Finlay's Casebook*, was filmed, and in recent years its proximity to the highly populated central belt has made it very popular among day trippers.

INFORMATION

Distance: 7 km (4 miles).

Start and finish: Car park on the south side of the main street, opposite the Dreadnought Hotel.

Terrain: Mostly on footpaths; some of these can be quite boggy in wet weather. walking boots or wellies are advised. **Part of the walk crosses the Callander Golf Course, and great care should be taken not to disrupt the play of the golfers.**

Time: Allow 2½–3 hours.

Refreshments: There are many restaurants, tea-rooms, cafes and pubs in Callander.

Attractions: The Rob Roy and Trossachs Visitor Centre is well worth visiting.

St Kessog's Church, now a very fine information centre.

Despite its popularity with those who want to visit the Highlands, Callander itself is very much a lowland town. It consists of a long, broad main street from which narrower streets and lanes run south towards the River Teith which forms its southern boundary. The first bridge across the river was built in 1764 and was replaced by the present bridge in 1907.

Those who experience some irritation at the crowds who flock to this town during holidays and weekends will perhaps sympathise with the poet John Keats who passed through Callander in 1818, describing it as 'vexatiously full of visitors'. The person to blame, of course, was Sir Walter Scott whose novels and writings on the nearby Trossachs, particularly the long romantic poem *The Lady of the Lake*, caught the imagination of the 19th-century public. They flocked to Callander, and to Aberfoyle, to drink in the atmosphere of the Children of the Mist, Rob Roy Macgregor and the Celtic twilight.

This walk, and the next, offers the visitor a walk around the town making full use of the wonderful woodlands which surround it, as well as its delightful golf course, and the former Callander–Oban railway.

As for the Callander Craigs walk, return to the Main Street and follow it along, across the bridge, to Tulipan Crescent. Turn into the Crescent, taking the first footpath on the left just before the tennis courts. Follow this path into the trees and turn right at the signpost.

The signposted route into the Callander woods.

Follow the paths through the lower woods and after 15–20 minutes of delightful woodland walking the footpath will merge with a surfaced forest road just before a large car park. Go through the car park, turn left onto the tarmac road and follow it for about 100m before turning right at a sign which says, 'To the walk round the Golf Course'.

This is a very narrow and overgrown footpath through bracken. After 50 m or so the path stops, so turn left and follow an even more ill-defined path for a short distance to a rusting kissing gate. Go through it and stick with a faint path, with the golf course appearing on your right.

Callander golf course.

Pass the 2nd tee, and follow the path which leads into the woods again. After a short distance the path leaves the woods and runs out onto the 7th tee. Pass the tee and keep to the left of the fairway, go over the brow of the hill and look for a lochan on your left through the trees. Just in front of the loch you'll come across another footpath so follow it alongside the 7th fairway for a short distance until you reach a prominent tractor path. Turn left onto this path and follow it across the 10th fairway. You'll then pass some birches on your right with two Scots pines on your left. Continue straight ahead towards some gorse bushes, cross to the 14th tee and turn right, heading for a prominent Scots pine. Go left before you reach the tree, cross the boundary wall, turn right and follow the path beside the wall for about 150 m.

Where the boundary wall suddenly turns left, go through an obvious gap in the wall and follow the path through some bracken with bungalows ahead of you. Turn right immediately behind the bungalows, and follow this footpath for 100m. Go straight over the crossroads and continue straight on. When the path abuts the main road, turn left and follow it for 100 m until it reaches the main Stirling–Callander road.

Turn right and follow this road back into Callander, passing the old church which now hosts the Rob Roy Exhibition, and back to the car park opposite the Dreadnought Hotel.

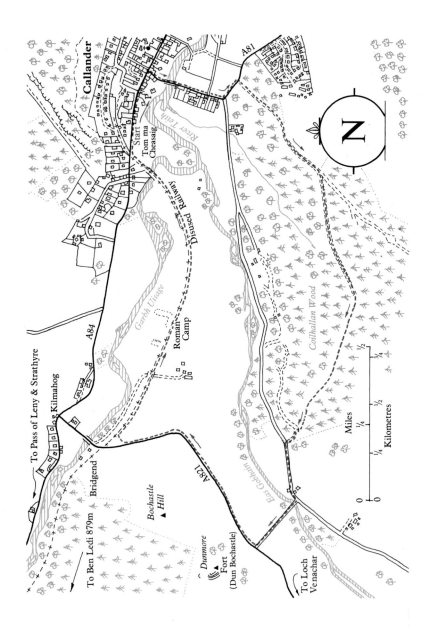

CALLANDER TOWN WALK 2

The car park is on an area known locally as The Meadows. Situated on the banks of the River Teith, it's a lovely spot with hundreds of ducks, all eager to be fed.

Go left (east) alongside the river, through a gap in the wall which gives access to a children's playground. The prominent mound on your right is quite ancient. It is called Tom na Cheasaig, commemorating St Cessoc, and the old Statistical Account claims that here, 'the people upon Sabbath evenings, exercised themselves with their bows and arrows, according to an ancient Scotch law for that purpose'. No bows and arrows nowadays, but how that thought would thrill so many of the youngsters who slide down that little hummock during the summer evenings.

Go through the playground and out of its far side onto the A81. Turn right, and cross the bridge on the narrow pavement (watch out for oncoming vehicles). There are good views of Ben Ledi from this point, with the River Teith as a fine foreground. This is a particularly good view in winter when the hill is swathed in white and the river may be partly frozen over.

INFORMATION

Distance: 7 km (4½ miles).

Start and finish: Car park opposite the Dreadnought Hotel.

Terrain: Mostly easy although some of the woodland walking can be muddy in wet weather. Walking boots or wellies are advised.

Time: About 2–3 hours.

Points of Interest: The Mound of Tom na Cheasaig at the start of the walk, the site of the ancient Dun Bochastle, the old Callander to Lochearnhead railway, now an excellent walkway, and the site of an old Roman camp.

Refreshments: Hotels, cafés and restaurants in Callander.

The start of the walk by the River Teith.

Continue past some houses and soon the road swings abruptly to the left. Follow it around the bend for about 100 m and then turn right, through two stone pillars, into some woodland. Follow the path slightly uphill, with a wire fence on your right, through a gate, then slightly left as the path continues to climb gradually. Follow this path, keeping the edge of the woodland firmly in your sight on the left. One or two other paths lead off to the right, but ignore them and keep the edge of the woodland on your left.

Soon, you'll notice more woods on your left. When you come level with them you'll find an old stone dyke leading off to the right. Follow the path which runs alongside the left of this dyke, a muddy and at times quite faint path. Continue on the path, deep into the woods, crossing some fallen trees and windblown scrub until your way ahead is barred by another wall, crossing the first wall at right angles. On your right you'll notice a gap in the original wall, so go through it and continue straight ahead below the spreading branches of an enormous beech tree for about 25–30 m before turning left again. The path is very faint here, but you will be walking through a gap in the trees; it would be exaggeration to call it a fire-break, but it's an obvious gap nevertheless.

Soon the path becomes very broken and rutted but you should be able to follow it without too much difficulty. Stay with it, weaving below the trees until you reach an obvious natural clearing on your left. Here the path swings to the right and drops down to

The waters of Eas Gobhain.

converge with a double rutted forest track. It's very rough, and very muddy in wet weather, but follow it down the short distance to the forestry car park at Coilhallan Wood. Turn left out of the car park, on to a tarmac road, with the rectangular, artificial ponds of the Trossachs Trout Farm in front of you.

Follow the tarmac road past some small cottages and turn right at the sign which indicates the A821 Trossachs road. Cross the bridge over the Eas Gobhain, an outflow of Loch Vennachar, and follow this straight road with bramble bushes (you can make a real pig of yourself here in season) on the verge on your right.

As you walk along this road you'll notice two hills in front of you, Dunmore on the left, and Bochastle Hill on the right, with its great boulder, a glacial erratic, dumped on its summit by some glacier many, many thousands of years ago. The boulder is known locally as Samson's Putting Stone. Although you can't really see anything of it nowadays, there was once a fort on Dunmore Hill, Dun Bochastle, possibly a strong fortress of the Pictish people.

At the end of the road, turn right along the A821. There is a good footpath on the left (north) side of the road, so follow it, below Bochastle Hill, with the views of Callander opening up to the right, the spire of St Kessog's Church being clearly visible.

Bochastle Hill, site of an old Iron Age fort.

Just before you reach the hamlet of Kilmahog, you'll come across a signpost on the roadside indicating a picnic area. Cross the road, and join the walkway adjacent to the picnic area. This was formerly the route of the Callander to Lochearnhead railway line (closed in 1964) and is nowadays a fine cycletrack and walkway which runs from Callander, through the Pass of Leny to Strathyre. Follow it under the old road bridge, and continue towards Callander. Soon you'll pass a field on your left with some strange low ridges in it. This is the site of an old Roman camp, a temporary camp as the might of the Roman legions never managed to quell the Scots to the north of the Antonine Wall.

Continue on the walkway all the way back into Callander, staying close to the river, where the path takes you back to the car park at The Meadows.

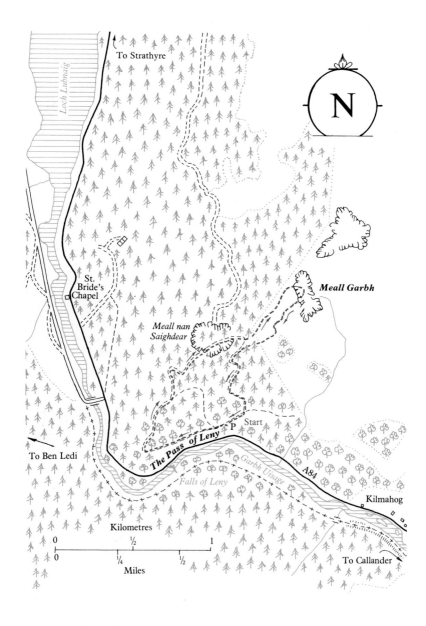

To Strathyre

Loch Lubnaig

N

St.
Bride's
Chapel

Meall Garbh

Meall nan
Saighdear

To Ben Ledi

P   Start

The Pass of Leny

Garbh Uisge

A84

Falls of Leny

Kilmahog

Kilometres

0   ½   1

0   ¼   ½

Miles

To Callander

THE PASS OF LENY AND MEALL GARBH

Few viewpoints exhibit the dramatic contrast between highland and lowland Scotland as well as this lovely view from the summit of Meall Garbh, a small hill situated above the Pass of Leny, north-west of Callander. The Pass itself is often regarded as a 'gateway to the highlands' for north of it the character of the landscape changes dramatically from rolling agricultural land to wild rocky outcrops and high mountains, with the eastern slopes of Ben Ledi louring over the narrow glen which holds Loch Lubnaig.

You may wish to visit the Falls of Leny before starting the walk to Meall Garbh – you can see them by crossing the A84, but take care as this road is normally very busy.

At the back of the car park a signpost points out the Forest Walks. The route is not immediately obvious as it wanders uphill beneath some very large and impressive Douglas firs but it soon becomes clearer. This is an old charcoal burners' track – local folk used to burn the oak into charcoal. You'll notice here and there large flat platforms, built up by stones and rocks, where the fires would have been.

Climb steadily up the hillside; the path soon begins to level out to hug the steep slope. Pass the charcoal burners' platforms and enjoy these wonderful oak woods. In spring and summer the place is vibrant with birdsong. Continue on the narrow path, which climbs steadily, and soon you'll see some prominent boulders on your left, and the first viewpoint of the walk – along the length of the Pass of Leny towards Callander and the lowlands. The name Leny is derived from the Gaelic word *lanaigh*, which surprisingly means 'boggy meadow'. The landscape in front of you contrasts with the mountainous terrain behind you, and the Pass of Leny is like an artery joining lowland and highland Scotland together.

Once you've drunk your fill of the view, return to the track and continue to follow it uphill. This really is a delightful section of footpath, clinging to the slope,

INFORMATION

Distance: 4 km (2½ miles) with about 300 m of ascent.

Start and finish: Falls of Leny car park on A85, 3 km north of Callander.

Terrain: A great variety of underfoot conditions from steep rocky paths to wet and slippy sections of path. Boots recommended.

Time: Give yourself a good 2–3 hours for this walk, bearing in mind some of the steep uphill sections involved.

Refreshments: Hotels, cafés and restaurants in Callander. There is a tea-room at Kilmahog.

Narrow snaking footpaths lead to the summit of Meall Garbh.

Ben Ledi from the Meall
Garbh track.

The descent from the summit
of Meall Garbh with
Callander in the distance.

and meandering upwards through the bent and twisted oaks. Near the top of the hill a signpost indicates a sharp right turn in the path. Take care here as there is an obvious natural viewpoint just to the left of the signpost, but it is quite exposed and potentially quite dangerous.

Just after the signpost the path enters a stand of conifers – compare the atmosphere of the dark and gloomy conifer woods with the delightful light oakwoods you have just left. The conifers only last a short while. Enter a firebreak with sitka spruce on either side.

Another firebreak leads to a division of the ways. Continue straight ahead if you want to return to the car park, but for those who feel like a bit of a climb and don't mind some steeper slopes, a signpost indicates the path to Meall Garbh – the wee pine-covered hill you can see ahead of you.

After a muddy start the path begins to contour the hillside, through some more lovely oakwoods. After a long uphill stretch, fallen pines block the path. Go round them on the right, cross a small drainage channel, then immediately turn left again to regain the path.

Carry on up another steep and fairly muddy section and reach a clear bealach, with good views of Ben Ledi and the Strathyre road far below you. Close beside the road lie the remains of St Bride's Chapel. According to Scott's *Lady of the Lake* this was the scene of a sad parting between a newly betrothed couple. In the story, the hero 'Angus, heir of Duncan's line' ran down from the heights of Ben Ledi with the Fiery Cross in his hand. He had been sent to summon the clan to battle and he, having run a fair stint from Lendrick on the banks of Loch Vennachar, was due to hand the burning emblem over to Norman of Ardnandave. Unfortunately, that young man had been married only moments before. As he escorted his bride from the Gothic arch of the chapel, his thoughts were far from running alongside Loch Lubnaig with a cross in his fist.

> With virgin steps and bashful hand,
> She held the kerchief's snowy band,
> The gallant bridegroom by her side,

Beheld his prize with Vistor's pride,
And the glad mother in her ear,
Was closely whispering words of cheer,
But, who meets them at the churchyard gate?

None other than bold Angus, soaking wet and bedraggled after swimming across the foaming River Leny. And so poor Norman, loyal to his clan, bade his new wife goodbye and set off at a run, cross in hand.

From the bealach climb up through some trees to a rocky knoll. The path more or less follows the line of an old rusting fence for a short distance before pulling away to the right. Continue the upwards climb and near the summit, as the path leaves the trees for a bit, a little spur with a large rock on top of it offers fine views south over the Menteith Hills to the Gargunnock and Fintry Hills.

Return to the path and climb to the summit of the hill. The views are extensive; beyond Callander to Stirling with the Castle and the Wallace Monument standing out clearly against the outline of the Ochil Hills. Beyond Stirling the red flames of the Grangemouth oil complex can often be seen and beyond them, the dim outline of the Pentland Hills.

From the summit, descend in the direction of Callander and as you enter the trees again follow the sign which indicates 'Forest Walk'. Drop downhill, with the fence on your left, until a signpost points to a turn to the right, back into the conifers. Pass a huge upturned root – there is a lot of storm damage hereabouts, but the path is quite clear.

Soon the path twists and turns as it descends through some scrubby birch. Here and there it becomes a bit slippery, so take care. Further down you run into a great jumble of windblown debris; pick your way carefully through it before dropping down through more oakwoods.

The path improves greatly now as it twists and turns its way down through the oaks back to the car park.

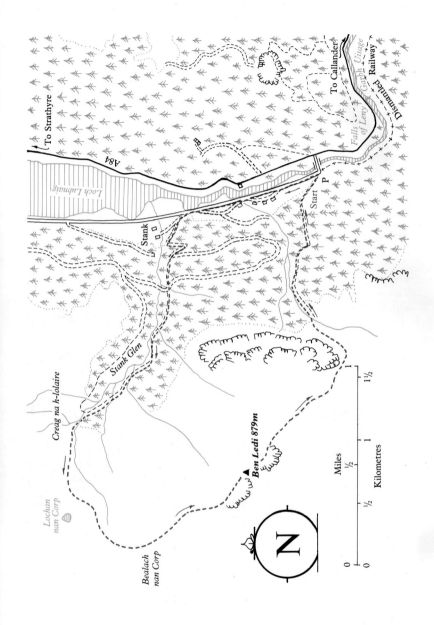

To Strathyre

A84

Loch Lubnaig

To Callander

Falls of Leny

Garbh Uisge

Railway

Dismantled

Stank

Start

P

Stank Glen

Creag na h-Iolaire

Ben Ledi 879m

Lochan nan Corp

Bealach nan Corp

N

Miles

½

1

1½

Kilometres

½

1

½

0

0

BEN LEDI

This fine hill, rising to 879 m/2883 ft, dominates the eastern Trossachs and can be seen to advantage from the bridge over the River Teith in Callander. The name of the hill has for long been a subject of dispute among Gaelic scholars and according to the old Scottish writer Seton Gordon, is taken from its Gaelic name of Beinn Lididdh, stressed on the first syllable. The somewhat picturesque derivation, Beinn le-Dia, the Hill of God, first suggested in an old Statistical Account, finds little favour among contemporary Gaelic scholars. It may be of some interest though, to quote the old account on the matter:

> By reason of the altitude of Ben Ledi and of its beautiful conical figure, the people of the adjacent country, to a great distance, assembled annually on its top, about the time of the summer solstice, during the Druidical priesthood, to worship the Deity. This assembly seems to have been a provincial or synodical meeting, wherein all the different congregations within the bounds wished to get as near to heaven as they could, to

INFORMATION

Distance: 11 km (7 miles), with 800 m ascent.

Start and finish: About 2 km north of Kilmahog on the A84 a left turn takes you over the river just beyond the Falls of Leny. Just beyond the bridge there is a good parking area.

Terrain: Mountain walking with a typical variety of underfoot conditions ranging from forest roads to deep peat. Some of the terrain is steep and great care is necessary. In misty conditions it is imperative that walkers can use a map and compass. Take OS 1:50000 Landranger map sheet 57.

Time: 6–8 hours.

Refreshments: None. It is important to carry adequate food and a hot drink.

Leaving the forest behind and onto the upper slopes of Ben Ledi.

pay their homage to the God of heaven. Tradition says that this devotional meeting continued three days. The summit of the mountain is smoothed and free of stones; which seems to be the work of art. But no stones with inscriptions can be found within the vicinity of that place.

The root of the name Beinn le-Dia is apparently the same as that of Beltane, the ancient Celtic festival which marked the coming of spring. On the first day of May, which was the Celtic New Year, people from the surrounding settlements and even further afield would climb Ben Ledi to light the beltane fire and greet the spring, the season of warmth and new life.

Take the left hand road from the car park, past some cottages including one called 'The Mancunian'. It belongs to a man from that part of the world who is a fine clarinettist.

After a mile or so the road degenerates into a track and runs to the farmhouse called Stank. Don't walk as far as the farmhouse but just before it take the forest road which runs off to the left. At a sharp hairpin bend look out for a green waymark on a rock opposite you which shows the start of the path up the Stank Glen. Follow this path as it twists sharply uphill through the trees to a point where it overlooks a very fine waterfall.

The forest hereabouts is subject to virtually constant change as great blocks of trees are clear felled and then replanted. The idea is to provide a rotating crop on a sustained basis, and the Forestry Commission has produced landscape design plans for this forest as far ahead as the year 2025, aimed at providing a mix of trees of different ages and species.

Ben Ledi.

Continue on the Stank Glen track to a height of about 450 m/1500 ft where you leave the main forest and step out into the upper glen. Your route slants half left up the hill, staying left of Creag na h-Iolaire (Crag of the Eagles). Continue past the crag onto the ridge and a little way to the north you'll come across Lochan nan Corp. This is an interesting little lochan, very much part of the local mythology. 'Corp' means body, and the lochan lies on an ancient coffin route, used to transport bodies from the glens to the west and down to St Bride's Chapel near the Pass of Leny. Local legend claims that once, when a funeral party was crossing the high ridge, they inadvertently crossed over the lochan, it being covered with ice and snow. The ice cracked open and some of the mourning party drowned in the freezing waters.

Once on the ridge, the way to the summit is straightforward: turn south and follow the line of old fenceposts which once marked the boundary between estates. The summit itself is a fine place to pause; crowned with an OS trig pillar it has remarkably wide vistas, from the jagged hills of the Isle of Arran in the south-west to the mighty Cairngorms in the north-east.

Ben Ledi.

From the subsidiary top a few hundred feet below the main summit you'll enjoy the grand prospect of the Highland Edge laid out before you. The descent continues abruptly down the ridge until the angle eases at some rather marshy ground. It then swings sharply left to cross a stile at the top of the forest. The footpath continues through the forest beside a small burn, and carries you all the way back down to the car park where you started.

This is right on the line of the former Stirling–Crianlarich railway, and what a super train ride that must have been, up through the forest and alongside Loch Lubnaig to Strathyre and Lochearnhead before the long pull up Glen Ogle towards Glen Dochart. It follows the line of an even older road, constructed in the 18th century as part of the network developed by General Wade and Major Caulfeild after the Jacobite uprisings.

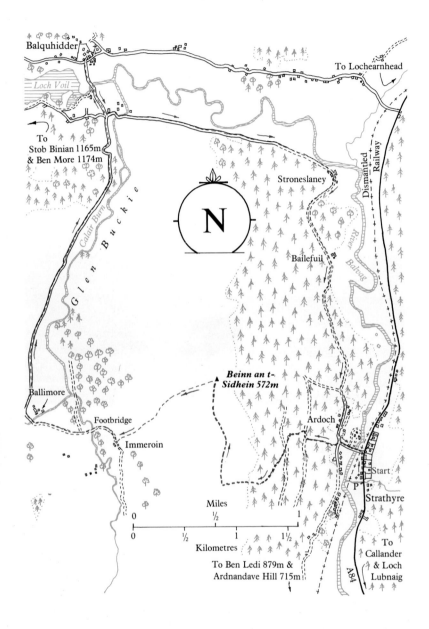

BEINN AN T-SIDHEIN

Beinn an t-Sidhein, the *Hill of the Faeries*, dominates the village of Strathyre. This small forestry village, the *Bonnie Strathyre* of the song, lies at the head of Loch Lubnaig on the A85 Callander–Lochearnhead road, and was once known as Nineveh on account of its large number of pubs!

The original crofting village of Strathyre was once on the other side of the River Balvag, but that was lost almost completely when the Callander–Oban railway was built. Time goes on, and now the railway is no more, the original track offering a fine walking route all the way from Callander, through Strathyre and Lochearnhead and over Glen Ogle to Killin.

It would have been a rather strange injustice if, in 1846, the Glasgow Water Company had fulfilled its plan of taking forty million gallons of water a day from Loch Lubnaig. This would have meant flooding the village of Strathyre. But, in the nick of time, the Company's works were taken over by the then Glasgow Corporation, who decided that Loch Katrine better suited their plans.

Strathyre may have been saved but it seems that some of our Gaelic names may have been lost. It's possibly an indication of the unfortunate trend in anglicising the old Gaelic names that the Forestry Commission have insisted in signposting Beinn an t-Sidhein as Ben Shian, or that a hotel in Strathyre is called the Ben

INFORMATION

Distance: 13 km (8 miles).

Start and finish: Car park, Strathyre village.

Terrain: A steep climb up Beinn an t-Sidhein, but on a good path. The track across the ridge is faint in places and not well waymarked, so take care. From Ballimore the rest of the walk is on a quiet tarmac road.

Time: 4–5 hours.

Refreshments: Hotels and tea-room in Strathyre. Public toilets in Strathyre.

Beinn an t-Sidhein.

Sheann Hotel. In the long run this trend fails to help visitors to understand the meaning of the Gaelic. The word Sith meaning fairy, is a word that hillwalkers and ramblers come across quite often and derivations such as Shian or Sheann only confuse the issue, and reduce the colourful, and often beautiful, Gaelic names to nondescript aberrations.

This walk offers a steep, but easy hill bash, lifting you quickly high above the village with a particularly fine view down the glen over Loch Lubnaig. Half of the distance comprises a return to Strathyre on a tarmac road but you are very unlikely to be pestered by cars or other vehicles. There is also an optional diversion into the tiny village of Balquhidder, the final resting-place of Rob Roy.

Loch Lubnaig from the slopes of Beinn an t-Sidhein.

From the car park, walk north through the village and turn left opposite the Munro Hotel. Cross the bridge over the Balvag, pass the Order of St John Home then turn left at the Forestry Commission signpost. A few metres beyond the signpost a footpath leaves the road on the right, and climbs steeply through the trees.

Climb straight uphill and after a while the track bends left, climbs up another steep stretch, and reaches a forest road. Go right on to the road, follow it for 100 m then turn left on to another footpath which is marked by a green/blue/white marker post. Climb uphill again with ever-widening views opening up along the valley to Loch Lubnaig and Ben Ledi. Soon you leave the views behind you as you enter the trees again and begin the steepest part of the ascent. It's hard work, but it doesn't last too long.

Take care at the top of this steep section where a rock slab appears to bar further progress. You can either climb over the slab, or turn it on the left, but take care because there is a steep drop below you. A little further on a track leads off to the right to Bailefuil. Ignore this sign and take the path which leads off diagonally left. Follow it out of the trees and on to the open moorland.

Signpost close to the start of the walk.

The path now crosses the broad south ridge of Beinn an t-Sidhein, with wonderful views south over the length of Loch Lubnaig with Ardnandave Hill and Ben Ledi rising from its western shore. Continue over the ridge, following the obvious footpath through the heather. As you begin to descend westwards great views begin to open up across Gleann Dubh, with the twin Munro peaks of Stobinian and Ben More rising above the hills in front of you.

Descend all the way to the farm at Immeroin, cross the river by the footbridge and continue through Glen Buckie to cross the Calair Burn by another bridge. On the north side of this bridge follow the tarmac track northwards, past the farm buildings of Ballimore. Follow the road down Glen Buckie, and if you like, continue across the River Balvag to visit Balquhidder and its famous churchyard which contains the burial place of Rob Roy, his wife and two sons.

Behind the village lie the slopes of the Braes of Balquhidder, celebrated in Robert Tannahill's song of the same name. There is a fine view from the bridge which crosses the River Balvag, near Loch Voil which is well worth a stop to enjoy it. Loch Voil has tiny wooded islands, promontories winding into the water and on both banks steep-sided hills stretch back, fold upon fold, becoming paler and paler into the jumble of high mountains which fade into the far west.

At the foot of Glen Buckie, bear right on the public road for the 6 km walk back to Strathyre. Although a tarmac road, this particular stretch is little used by cars and offers a fine, quiet and leisurely walk past Stroneslaney, Bailefuil and Ardoch to Strathyre.

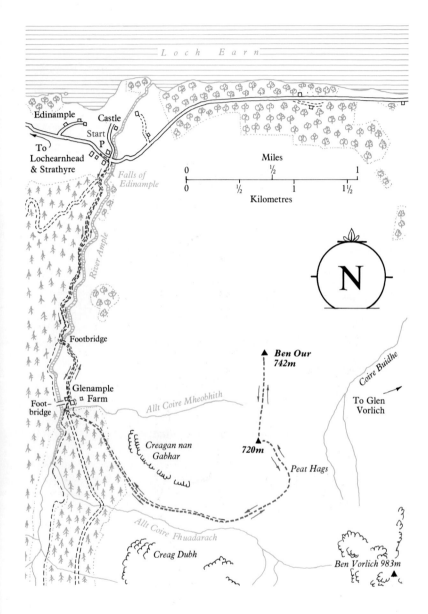

Loch Earn

Edinample

Castle

Start
P

To
Lochearnhead
& Strathyre

Falls of
Edinample

Miles

0 ½ 1

0 ½ 1 1½

Kilometres

River Ample

N

▲ Ben Our
742m

Coire Buidhe

To Glen
Vorlich

Footbridge

Glenample
Farm

Foot-
bridge

Allt Coire Mheobhith

Creagan nan
Gabhar

720m

Peat Hags

Allt Coire Fhuadarach

Creag Dubh

Ben Vorlich 983m ▲

BEN OUR

This little hill, known locally as Ben Or, means the 'Hill of Gold'. Rising above Loch Earn it offers dramatic views of the big hills around it – Ben Vorlich, the Lawers group, and the Braes of Balquhidder. It offers a pleasant outing for surprisingly little energy expenditure and gives the flavour of a real mountain walk.

INFORMATION

Distance: 13 km (8 miles) with 700 m ascent.

Start and finish: The South Loch Earn road, a little less than a mile from its junction with the main A84 Strathyre– Lochearnhead road. As you drive along this road you'll pass a white castle on your left – Edinample, the erstwhile home of the Marquis of Breadalbane. Not far beyond the castle you'll reach some houses and a small church. Park your car before crossing the bridge over the River Ample.

Terrain: Good walking boots are advised; although this is not a serious mountain walk it is wet and boggy in places underfoot. A map (OS Landranger sheet 51) and compass should be carried.

Time: Give yourself about 4–5 hours.

Refreshments: None.

River Ample

From the parking area, a track leads off to the right following the waters of the River Ample. Beyond the waterfalls, the Falls of Edinample, which can be impressive after times of heavy rain, the track bends to the left to a gate. Take the left fork here and follow the track which runs close to the river. Continue on this route for about 1.5 km, until the track crosses the river over a bridge. Leave the hard-surfaced track here and take a footpath which runs along a grassy verge between the river and a deer fence on your right. Cross the river again by a small wooden bridge.

Ben Our across Loch Earn

Follow the deer fence on your left with the buildings on the opposite side. The path bears left and crosses a burn where a fencepost is marked with arrows. Follow the red arrow, turn left up a a small embankment and on to another track (which in fact comes out of Glenample Farm). Turn right on to this track and continue uphill, away from the farm.

Continue on this track, through a young plantation, and follow the route up by an old fence towards a more recent deer fence. A stile takes you over this fence and on to an old track. Follow this track uphill, with good views beginning to open up around you. On your left, the big open slopes of Creagan nan Gabhar and Coire Mheobhith lead to the double-topped summit slopes of Ben Our, while below you Glen Ample stretches its way back towards Loch Earn.

Keep climbing steadily and soon the summit of Ben Vorlich appears in front of you, high and impressive. Shortly after this the track suddenly stops, at a height of around 550 m. Climb the open slope beyond the end of the track in a leftwards direction. There is a faint path but it may be difficult to find. Keep to the rising slope though, and soon you'll reach the broad ridge, with Coire Buidhe ('yellow corrie') falling away to your right. The ridge itself is covered with peat hags, so try to keep to the left of them as you climb to the first summit. The main peak lies about 800 m to the north, and it's an easy walk across the high moorland ridge.

If the conditions are clear, take your time at the summit and enjoy to the full the magnificent panorama of mountains and lochs all around you. Return the way you came.

Falls, Glen Ample

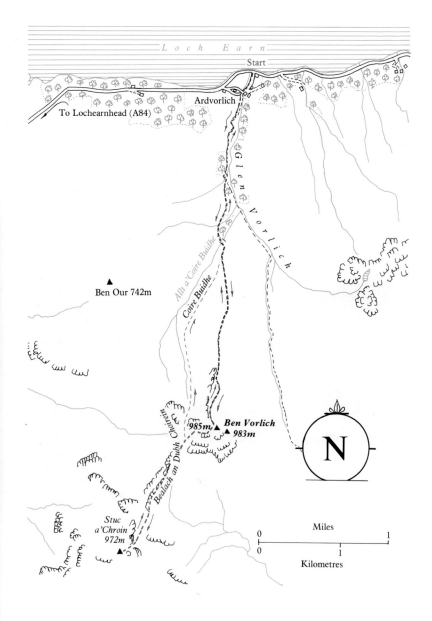

Loch Earn

Start

Ardvorlich

To Lochearnhead (A84)

Glen Vorlich

Allt a'Coire Buidhe

Coire Buidhe

Ben Our 742m

985m ▲ **Ben Vorlich**
▲ 983m

Bealach an Dubh Choirein

Stuc a'Chroin 972m

N

Miles
0   1

0   1
Kilometres

BEN VORLICH

Not to be confused with the Ben Vorlich which frowns down on the head of Loch Lomond, this Perthshire Ben Vorlich shares the same name origin. It comes from the gaelic *Mur-Bhalg,* meaning 'sea-bay', and refers to small bays in the lochs which sit at their respective feet. Ardvorlich, at the beginning of this hill walk, is therefore Ard-Mhurlaig, the Promontory of the Sea-bay, and is the home of the Stewarts of Ardvorlich, an ancient family who have held these lands for some 400 years.

For many years a stone was kept in Ardvorlich House, the Clach Dearg, or 'Red Stone', which was believed to have miraculous properties. If you dipped it in a pail of water and moved it three times sun-wise around the pail, the water would then contain healing powers which could be used to treat sick cattle. So famous was this stone that it attracted people from all around the area, who came with their own buckets to carry home some of the miraculous water which had been swilled over the stone. It was said that the stone had been brought back to Ardvorlich House in the 14th century after a crusade.

Beyond the house, away up Glen Vorlich lie the high slopes of Ben Vorlich, at 985 m/3232 ft one of Scotland's 277 Munros, or mountains over the height of 914 m/3000 ft. The hills of the Trossachs are generally smaller and Ben Vorlich is the only Munro described in this book. As such, it should be noted that its ascent, while straightforward enough for experienced hillwalkers, is a considerable undertaking for those who normally walk low-level routes. Its height above sea level shouldn't be underestimated, as bad weather can come in at any time of the year. Anyone attempting this walk should be well equipped and should be able to use a map and a compass.

Take the private road from the east gate of Ardvorlich House on the south side of Loch Earn. As you enter through the gates of the estate follow the road south, past the farm, where a signpost points to the right. Cross a stone bridge, and find another sign, this time pointing to the left. The track now wanders up

Ben Vorlich and
Stuc a' Chroin.

through Glen Vorlich, a lovely spot with a tree-lined burn and good views opening up across Loch Earn towards the mighty Lawers hills.

Just over 1.5 km further on, a wooden bridge crosses the Allt a' Coire Buidhe ('burn of the yellow corrie'). The real walking begins now, a stony footpath which heads right across the bare moorland and begins to climb onto the steeper and stonier north-east ridge of Ben Vorlich itself.

The path is clear and obvious and climbs delightfully up this ridge with wonderful views opening up in all directions. Stop and gaze behind you from time to time and enjoy the panorama across Loch Earn. The Ben Lawers hills and the Tarmachans stand out against the northern skyline with a jumble of mountains beyond them. Further west the Braes of Balquhidder form a foreground to the higher hills beyond, the long ridge of Stobinian and the even higher cone of Ben More above Crianlarich.

Continue upwards on the stony path to the summit ridge, which is about 100 m long. The OS trig pillar is at its north-west end, with a cairn at the other end. The trig pillar signifies the summit.

Hillwalkers, particularly those collecting Munros, will want to add the ascent of Stuc a' Chroin, Vorlich's neighbouring Munro, to their day's climb. While the ascent of Stuc a' Chroin from Ben Vorlich is straightforward enough, it does involve some fairly exposed scrambling from the adjoining Bealach an Dubh Choirein ('pass of the black corrie').

The steeper ground can be avoided by ascending in a south-westerly direction from the bealach, avoiding the obvious rocky buttress by traversing about 15 m to the right (north-west) and following a steep path up through broken rocks. The direct route up the north-east buttress offers fine scrambling for those used to such things, but is definitely not for the inexperienced. At the top of the buttress you'll reach a small cairn, and the summit of Stuc a' Chroin is only a couple of hundred metres away along a line of fence posts.

To return to Ardvorlich from Stuc a' Chroin, simply descend to the Bealach an Dubh Choirean and then traverse north across a grassy hillside to reach another bealach at the head of Coire Buidhe. Descend the east ridge of the corrie to regain the footpath in Glen Vorlich. To return from Ben Vorlich, retrace the outward route to Ardvorlich.

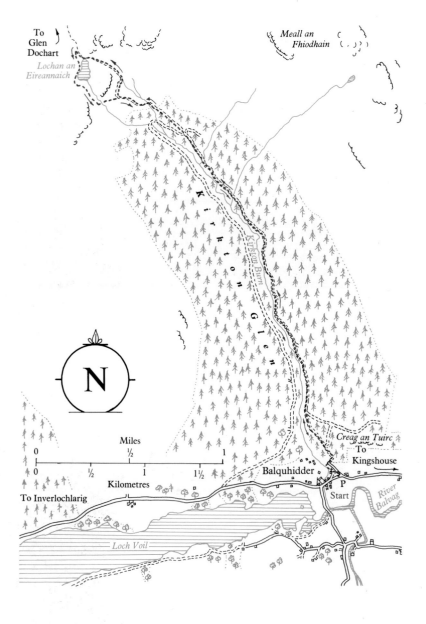

To
Glen
Dochart

*Lochan an
Eireannaich*

*Meall an
Fhiodhain*

Kirkton Burn

Kirkton Glen

N

Miles

0   ½   1

0   ½   1   1½

Kilometres

To Inverlochlarig

Loch Voil

Creag an Tuirc

To
Kingshouse

Balquhidder

P

Start

*River
Balvag*

KIRKTON GLEN

Drive along Balquhidder Glen from Kingshouse and you'll see before you a wonderful scene of mountain and loch. As the road rises above the River Balvag, the silver slash of Loch Voil in the distance forms a foreground to layer upon layer of mountain slopes. On both sides of the loch the hills rise steeply, and on an autumn day when the sun is dropping beyond the high hills of Beinn Tulaichain and Stob a' Choin at the far end of the glen you can begin to understand the magic of this place.

This was the view which inspired the poet Robert Tannahill to write his lovely *Braes o' Balquhidder* in the 18th century, a poem now remembered as the song, *Will ye go Lassie, go*. And it was here, while watching the girls from Balquhidder bringing in the harvest sheaves to the melody of Gaelic sons, that William Wordsworth was inspired to write his poem, *The Solitary Reaper*.

It's a romantic place, and in a sense wholly appropriate that it is also the final resting place of the area's most notable son, Rob Roy. Rob died at his farm of Inverlochlarig, at the far end of the Balquhidder glen, on 27 December 1734. It was a peaceful end to a daring and tumultuous life, and the story of his last hours have passed into legend. As he lay on his death bed, he was informed by his ghillie that MacLaren of Invernety, a traditional enemy, had come to pay his respects. Not wanting to be seen in his bedclothes, he commanded his family to dress him in his tartan plaid, belted with dirk and pistol, and sat in his chair. He thus greeted his visitor.

When the MacLaren left, Rob fell back exhausted and said, 'It is all over. Put me to bed. Call the piper and let him play *Cha till mi Tuille* (the lament "I Shall Return No More")'. Before the piper had completed the dirge, Rob had passed away. On New Year's Day 1735 his body was carried in great ceremony and mourning, preceded by the clan pipers, down the length of the glen to the tiny kirk at Balquhidder, where he was laid to rest, beneath his beloved Braes. So many people attended the funeral that it cost his family £400 Scots, an enormous sum in those days.

INFORMATION

Distance: 8 km (5 miles)

Start and finish: Balquhidder church on a minor road leading west from Kingshouse on the A85, north of Strathyre.

Terrain: Mostly forest tracks but some muddy footpaths higher up. Easy terrain but take care at the top of the pass for it can become misty very quickly. Boots or wellies recommended.

Time: 3–4 hours

Refreshments: None.

The crags of Meall an Fhiodhain above the Irishman's Loch.

Rob Roy's grave in
Balquhidder kirkyard.

Kirkton Glen lies behind the kirk of Balquhidder, and for centuries has been used as a through route between Balquhidder and Glen Dochart in the north. Even in Rob Roy's day it was used as an 'escape route' if enemy presence meant the Balquhidder glen became too hot for comfort.

It is possible to walk the full 12 km from Balquhidder through to Glen Dochart, catching a bus to bring you back to Kingshouse on the A85. Better to arrange for another car to meet you in Glen Dochart, or perhaps two parties could begin from either end, exchanging car keys when they meet in the middle. But for this walk I have described the walk from Balquhidder to Lochan an Eireannaich at the head of the pass, returning much the same way back to Balquhidder.

Start at the Balquhidder kirkyard, where it's worthwhile spending some time exploring the church and its fascinating graveyard. The church will be described more fully in the next walk. Rob Roy, his wife Helen and son Coll are buried here side by side. Rob's gravestone is an interesting one – it's reckoned to date from the 14th century, so it was ancient even in Rob Roy's day. It is carved with a warrior and a two-handed claymore.

Form the north-west corner of the churchyard a track leads into the forest. Follow this track, turning right at the signpost which indicates Kirkton Glen. If you carry straight on at this point you'll come to a bridge over the river beside some lovely waterfalls – well worth the short diversion.

Cross a stile at the rear of the church beside the Forest Enterprise signs which indicate the Kirkton Glen Walks and continue on the broad forest track as it begins to climb, bearing right, then left as it enters the conifers. Climb steeply through the trees, pass a huge area of clear-fell on your right and continue past the buildings on your right. Ignore the road which goes off to the right just after the buildings – this leads to Creag an Tuirc, the subject of the next walk.

Soon you'll reach another track coming in from the left over a bridge. Ignore this too and continue straight ahead for a good 2 km of forest walking, climbing gently all the way. The end of the forest road will be quite obvious; a large clear-felled area with the road looping hard to the right. Directly ahead of you a narrow and, at time of writing, faint footpath wanders through a clear-felled area before breaking free of the trees in the upper slopes. The path improves as you climb high and you'll reach a boundary fence where the path turns left to run for a short distance adjacent to the fence. Cross a burn and a few yards further on a stile takes you over the fence.

Once across the stile, the footpath is clearly defined over the rough, grassy slopes, climbing higher and eventually looping to the right to bring you below the frowning crags and boulders of Meall an Fhiodhain.

Balquhidder Kirk.

Trace your way through the fallen boulders at the foot of the cliff and make your way in a north-west direction to rejoin the main path beyond Lochan an Eireannaich. It's well worth continuing northwards for a distance for the view down into Glen Dochart before returning to the lochan.

Lochan an Eireannaich is in a lovely setting, a high grassy hollow with the frowning Meall an Fhiodhain making a wonderfully rugged backdrop. This is 'the small lochan of the Irishman', and the name goes back many hundreds of years. During the years of the Roman attempts at occupation, there began to be felt an Irish influence on the area, and the northern part of the district became known as Ath Fhodhla or New Ireland. (Fhodhla was a pagan queen of Ireland.) That area is nowadays known as Atholl. To the south and south-west of Ath Fhodhla were Strath Eireann (Strathearn) and Loch Eireann (Loch Earn), the Strath of Ireland and the Loch of Ireland.

The steep rocky crags of
Meall an Fhiodhain.

Early Irish immigrants were in the habit of naming their new home Ireland and the districts of the new settlements were usually named after Irish Districts. It's therefore not surprising there here we have a Small Loch of the Irishman here.

Follow the path around the loch, and follow the outflow of the loch down steeper grassy slopes to meet up with your approach path. Return to the fence and retrace your steps back to Balquhidder.

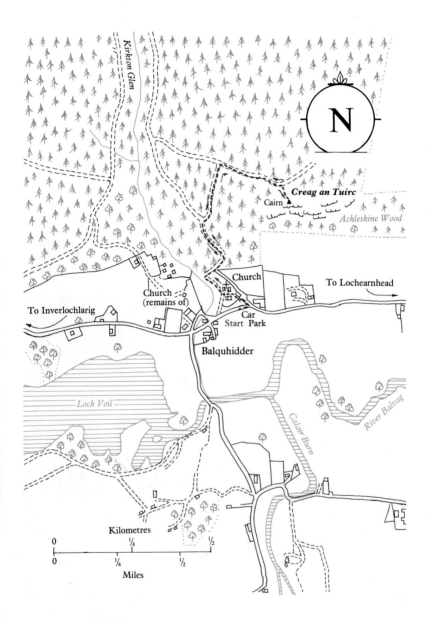

Kirkton Glen

N

Creag an Tuirc

Cairn

Achleskine Wood

Church

To Lochearnhead

Church
(remains of)

Car
Start Park

To Inverlochlarig

Balquhidder

Loch Voil

Calair Burn

River Balvag

Kilometres

| 0 | | ¼ | | ½ |

0   ¼   ½
Miles

CREAG AN TUIRC

This is a short but very pleasant walk onto a high bluff overlooking Balquhidder. Indeed the ease of the walk is not really commensurate with the wonderful panorama that is on offer from the top, one of the finest views in the surrounding area.

Like walk 23, this one begins from Balquhidder Church. The present building, built by David Carnegie of Stronvar, was opened in September 1855. The ruined church in the kirkyard bears the date 1631 and was built by David Murray, Lord Scone, whose initials appear above the doorway. It's built partly on top of the pre-Reformation Church and its bell, donated by its erstwhile minister, the Rev Robert Kirk (he of the faeries and elves) was used until 1895. It now lives on top of the Session Chest in the new church.

INFORMATION

Distance: 3 km (2 miles).

Start and finish: Balquhidder church, as walk 23.

Terrain: Easy walking, mostly on forest tracks.

Time: 1–2 hours, depending on how long you want to linger on the summit.

Refreshments: None.

Loch Voil stretching into the western hills.

The pre-Reformation church dates back to the 13th century, or possibly earlier. Some of its foundations can be seen near to Rob Roy's grave. It was known as Eaglais Beag ('Little Church') and it's thought it may have been built over the grave of St Angus. Indeed, the cell of St Angus was believed to have stood in the field below the Church. Old foundations were removed from there about 1860. A large stone, the St Angus Stone, believed to have lain over his grave, can be seen leaning against the north wall inside the present church. It is thought to date from 750–850AD.

The Balquhidder parish is the traditional home of the MacLarens and is also associated with the Balquhidder Fergussons, the Macgregors and the Stewarts of Glen Buckie. The object of this walk is to visit the gathering place of the Clan MacLaren, Creag an Tuirc, the Crag of the Boar, and the clan remain owners of the rock even to this day.

Like the Macgregors, the MacLarens knew turbulent times. They were staunch supporters of the Jacobite cause, and even after Culloden, they continued to bear arms and wear the White Cockade, the emblem of the Stuart cause. Each clan had a gathering place to where they were summoned by the Fiery Cross. This burning emblem would be carried by runners around the clan district, summoning the men to battle.

Clan MacLaren memorial on the summit of Creag an Tuirc.

Take the track at the back of the church signposted Kirkton Glen. Turn right behind the church, cross the stile and make your way up the forest track into the conifers. Climb steeply up this forest track until it emerges from the trees. A short distance beyond, it forks, just beyond some buildings which are enclosed in a wire fence. Take the right fork and continue on this track for some distance. Watch out for a sign on your right which leads to a small footpath which goes through a gap in a dry stone wall. Climb the slopes leading to the summit below some very fine Scots pines. There is a memorial cairn on the summit.

Spend some time here if you can, for the view is stunning. The 22 km length of the Balquhidder glen stretches out to your right, a series of overlapping mountain slopes, shade upon shade, dropping down to the long slit of Loch Voil and beyond it, Loch Doine.

The Clan memorial with Loch Voil stretching into the distance.

Away beyond Loch Doine lies the house of Inverlochlarig, where Rob Roy died, and a little bit closer, between the two lochs, the house of Monachyle Tuarach, where Rob and his wife Mary Macgregor of Comar (called Helen by Sir Walter Scott) first settled into married life.

An alternative descent route is possible from the summit, by following the signposts in a more direct route than that by which you approached. Unfortunately, a huge area of clear felling has made this a rather difficult ascent and any path which may have existed has been been well and truly obliterated. It's therefore best to return to Balquhidder churchyard by the outward route.

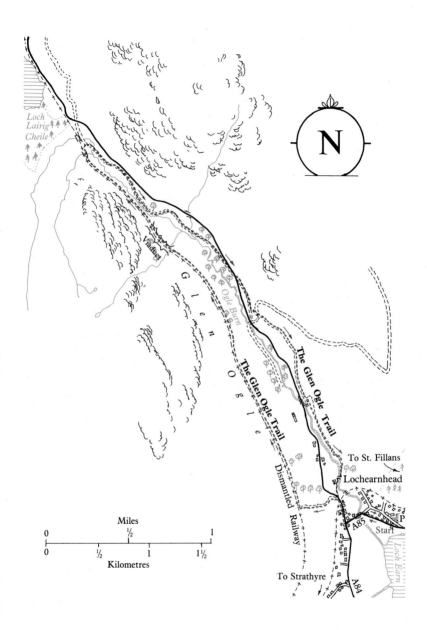

Loch
Lairig
Cheile

Viaduct

Ogle Burn

G
l
e
n

O
g
l
e

The Glen Ogle Trail

The Glen Ogle Trail

Dismantled Railway

N

To St. Fillans

Lochearnhead

A85

Start

P

Loch Earn

To Strathyre

A84

Miles

0   ½   1

0   ½   1   1½

Kilometres

THE GLEN OGLE TRAIL

Despite being a railway buff when I was a youngster, I've never quite shared the enthusiasts' passion for walking along old railway tracks. One which does offer an outstanding walk though is the old line between Lochearnhead up the length of Glen Ogle. This track makes up part of the Glen Ogle Trail, an imaginative walking route devised and made possible by an access agreement between Stirling District Council and local landowners.

The route ascends Glen Ogle from Lochearnhead following the trackbed of the old Caledonian Railway which once ran north from Stirling, via Callander and Strathyre, then westwards towards its final destination at Oban. The line was opened in 1880 and eventually closed in 1965.

The line it takes up Glen Ogle is an interesting one, running roughly parallel with the road built originally by that Irish road builder of the 18th century, Major Caulfeild. But travellers had been using Glen Ogle as a gateway to the highlands long before that. It's said that Roman legions once tramped this way as well as generations of drovers and travellers.

The start of this walking trail is by the old Lochearnhead railway station, now used as the local

INFORMATION

Distance: 8 km (5 miles).

Start and finish: Car park in Lochearnhead, opposite the watersports centre.

Terrain: Mostly easy walking after a steep start. Boots are advised, for the old trackbed can be quite rough in places.

Time: Allow about 3 hours, more if it's a good day and you can sit by the stream on the return journey down Glen Ogle.

Toilets: Public toilets adjacent to the main car park in Lochearnhead.

Refreshments: Restaurants and cafes in Lochearnhead.

Loch Earn. This view was once thought to be the finest view from a train in Britain.

Boy Scout headquarters. Interestingly enough, this old building wasn't on the original Caledonian Line but was a station on the Crieff-Lochearnhead line, which was closed in 1951. Both lines ran together as far as Balquhidder in the south, then the Caledonian Line took a much higher route before tackling the long and steady pull up Glen Ogle. This means that walkers have to climb from the former Lochearnhead Station to the start of the trackbed itself.

Cattle in Glen Ogle near the end of the walk.

From the car park, walk to the road junction of A84/A85, turn right and walk past the dismantled railway bridge. Just beyond here, cross over the road and turn left onto the driveway of the Lochearnhead Boy Scout Station. Almost immediately, a footpath leaves the drive to the right, at a sign which indicates the Glen Ogle Trail. Follow this footpath up through the trees, over a stile, across a gorse-covered field and up a series of wooden steps.

Continue uphill, over an old boundary wall, following the arrow signs which indicate the Glen Ogle Trail as the path zigzags back and forth. Continue the sharp climb for a short distance more to reach another stile. Before you cross it look back towards the view down the length of Loch Earn towards St Fillans, at one time thought to be the finest view from a railway anywhere in the country. It certainly is quite stunning, with the bulk of Ben Our dominating the upper reaches of the loch, and the Munro of Stuc a' Chroin looking quite Alpine in character.

Cross the stile and climb the steps which take you onto the old railway trackbed. The condition of the trackbed is excellent and offers a good, if occasionally rough, walking surface for its route up the glen. It crosses several old bridges and a well-preserved 12-arched viaduct.

Ancient Scots pines line much of the route – trees which would have seen the coming and the going of the railway, and younger scrub birches, most certainly grown since the closure of the railway, which meet overhead to form a green canopy above you – very welcome for the shade it offers on a hot day.

Follow the trackbed along its length, over the bridges and across the viaduct. Take care on this latter feature, as there is no retaining wall on the left. The edge of the track is crumbly is places, and it's a big drop below – so keep well to the centre of the track and you'll experience little difficulty.

The trail crosses this old viaduct three quarters of the way up Glen Ogle.

At the end of the trackbed you'll reach a fence and stile. Cross the stile on to a stretch of track which is in poor repair. Clamber along the right-hand side of the rubble for about 100 m until you come to a ladder stile. Cross it and drop down to the green track below you, which leads down to a little hump-backed bridge.

This marks the beginning of a lovely stretch of footpath, down the glen between the burn and the main road. Soon you'll reach a stretch of river well covered by alders, and not long after that the path runs close to the road for a short distance. Another ladder stile crosses a wall on to the road, which should then be crossed with care. On the opposite side of the road the path is well marked by a series of arrow markers and ladder stiles which carry you over a succession of fields running high above, but parallel to the main road.

As you walk down the glen you'll pass some buildings on their left side, and then the path drops down to run alongside the burn. A footbridge carries you over the burn, then a gate gives access to a field just past an electricity sub-station. At the far end of the field another ladder stile, or a gate to its left, gives access to the main road, from where you can walk back to the car park in Lochearnhead where you started.

INDEX

Other titles in this series

25 Walks – Deeside
25 Walks – Edinburgh and Lothian
25 Walks – In and Around Glasgow
25 Walks – Highland Perthshire

Other titles in preparation

25 Walks – In and Around Aberdeen
25 Walks – Dumfries and Galloway
25 Walks – Fife
25 Walks – The Scottish Borders

Long distance guides published by HMSO

The West Highland Way – Official Guide
The Southern Upland Way – Official Guide

HMSO publications are available from:

HMSO Bookshops
71 Lothian Road, Edinburgh EH3 9AZ
0131-228 4181 Fax 0131-229 2734
49 High Holborn, London WC1V 6HB
(counter service only)
0171-873 0011 Fax 0171-831 1326
68-69 Bull Street, Birmingham B4 6AD
0121-236 9696 Fax 0121-236 9699
33 Wine Street, Bristol BS1 2BQ
0117 9264306 Fax 0117 9294515
9-21 Princess Street, Manchester M60 8AS
0161-834 7201 Fax 0161-833 0634
16 Arthur Street, Belfast BT1 4GD
01232 238451 Fax 01232 235401

HMSO Publications Centre
(Mail, fax and telephone orders only)
PO Box 276, London SW8 5DT
Telephone orders 0171-873 9090
General enquiries 0171-873 0011
(queuing system in operation for both numbers)
Fax orders 0171-873 8200

HMSO's Accredited Agents
(see Yellow Pages)

and through good booksellers

Printed in Scotland for HMSO by CC No. 70343 50C 4/95